ROCK GARDENS

Rock Gardens

Douglas Bartrum

JOHN GIFFORD LIMITED
London

S.B.N. 70710402 5

Printed in Great Britain
by Cox and Wyman Ltd, London, Fakenham and Reading

Contents

ROCK GARDENS

Introduction

When did rock-gardening begin? The question (once asked me) sounds peremptory and perhaps a little odd. Many writers say round about 1870. Nobody knows when the first rock was laid and nobody has actually written much about the history of rock-gardening. It seems unimportant anyhow. Probably 'Capability' Brown (1716–83), one of our most famous landscape-gardeners, with his vision of greater freedom and naturalistic effects in layout and design, stimulated men's imagination and was instrumental in influencing designers to create new features such as the rockery, the water-garden and the like.* Of course we know that alpine plants, both from Europe and from other parts of the world had been introduced into Britain long before Brown's time—the Alpine Roses (Rhododendrons) R. *hirsutum* in 1656, and R. *ferrugineum*, later. These dwarf shrubs were probably grown mostly by nurseries or by collectors and planted in pots or set out in shrubberies. (Neither however does particularly well in cultivation).

One writer† says 'When the great age of formal gardening—which gave us the stately beauty of Chatsworth and Montacute—yielded place to the landscape era of "Capability" Brown, rock-gardening was born ... A gardening world which sought escape from the formality of parterres and clipped hedges, found relief in the so-called "natural" effect of great stone masses, waterfalls, grottoes and miniature Matterhorns.' Humphrey Repton (1752–1818), as well known as 'Capability' Brown, and the author of

* Lancelot Brown, born at Kirkharle, Northumberland, was nicknamed 'Capability' as the result of his fondness for stating that he could always see 'capabilities' in the estates he was commissioned to re-design and improve. It is said that he possessed a remarkable gift of visualizing the completed layout when viewing a prospective site; his prejudgements however were not always commendable.

† *The Shell Gardens Book* (Phoenix House, George Rainbird Ltd.), pages 168–9.

9

various works on landscape-gardening, advocated the use of rocks in the garden layout—'The contrasted greens of wood and lawn are not sufficient to gratify the eye; it requires other objects, and those of different colour, such as rocks, water . . .' (quoted from his *An Enquiry Into The Change Of Taste In Landscape Gardening* published in 1806).

But rocks in a garden didn't constitute a rockery. Rocks might easily be found as a natural feature in certain parts of the country, often by the side of a stream with plants growing near them. Rocks no doubt provided contrast and also a break in the sweeping grasslands and lawns, though a nicely placed drift of Heathers would have done the same just as effectually.

Contrary to some writers' belief, the rock-garden wasn't derived from any form of grotto: the grotto was an ornamental feature that was apparently very popular in the seventeenth century; it was a cave-like structure artificially built of rocks (often indigenous to the locality of the garden). Alexander Pope (1688–1744), the poet, a great garden lover, built a famous grotto in his garden at Twickenham, helped by William Kent and Charles Bridgeman, both adherents of the naturalistic school of landscape-gardening.

To return to our date 1870: this was the year of the publication of *Alpine Flowers for English Gardens* by William Robinson (1839–1935), and it seems that about this time more interest began to be taken in rock plants than ever before. More books, more magazines described rock plants and methods of building rockeries for small gardens. Charles McIntosh devotes a chapter to rock plants and ways of growing them on rock-work in his *The Flower Garden* published in 1838; *Florist's Journal* (1845) mentions a method of rockery construction on page 224. And much earlier than this in the *Botanical Magazine*, first published in 1781 by William Curtis (who originated the idea of such a publication) alpine plants figure quite frequently: in 1797 a charming plate and a description of the rare and very lovely white alpine Buttercup, *Ranunculus parnassifolius* from the Alps appeared; the plant was introduced into Britain about 1770. More descriptions, more illustrations, more plants introduced from the Alps and from other mountainous parts of the world. Botanic gardens were building rockeries—Kew began work on its famous rock-garden in 1882. By the end of the century rock-gardening had become as popular as many other branches of gardening and designers had come to regard the rockery as an important feature in the layout of the English pleasure garden.

CHAPTER I

Rockeries

A point not mentioned in the introduction but pertinent to the cultivation of alpines* in the garden is that they often need a special setting to show them off to best advantage. For example, a trailing plant such as the common but very beautiful double white *Arabis* requires a perpendicular boulder, down which it can trail and display its long stems carrying the flowers. The plant may, of course, be used (and often is used) as an edging plant for the flower border or in a formal bedding scheme (it was introduced in 1798). Most trailers, *Aubrietia*, 1710, and *Saponaria ocymoides*, 1768, to mention two special favourites, look best on vertical rock-work, or on wall-gardens that are built against earth banks as retaining-walls (holding up the earth or soil, see Chapter 3), or growing perhaps somewhere high up and showing off their mass of hanging flowers. On flat soil, say, in a flower-bed, they lose much of their character.

Other kinds of alpines growing in or near glacier detritus, some Gentians, for instance, such as the blue, velvety *Gentiana verna* should be planted in scree or moraine soil (leafy or sandy loam containing plenty of granite chips); and scree conditions can be provided only in a rockery or in an alpine garden, which is the same thing. You couldn't grow this glorious little Gentian in a flower border however much you tried.

And yet other kinds of alpines such as some of the Androsaces need overhanging rocks to protect their hairy foliage from excessive moisture: *A. imbricata* is one of these and is very difficult in cultivation (it isn't possible to grow it in every rock-garden and is more often than not given a pot or pan in the alpine house).

* Alpines: not only plants from the Alps of Europe: the word is now used to describe those plants that grow on mountains in all parts of the world.

Alpine Primulas need cool moist fissures and often deep shade best part of the day. Most difficult of all to grow perhaps are those plants that grow near the snow-line and are dormant for many months of the year. Impossible to reproduce alpine weather in our gardens. You might get heavy falls of snow and mountain mists in certain parts of Scotland, but comparatively few people have gardens in these mountainous districts and they would probably prefer to grow vegetables, anyway.

It might have been the botanic gardens that set the fashion. And no doubt the increasing number of alpine plants being introduced spurred them on. We learnt much from them; for these rockeries were expertly designed. And gardeners who study the experts' methods and layouts can scarcely go wrong.

Materials

Several kinds of rock or stone were used at Kew in the construction of the rock-garden. LIMESTONE from the Mendips (Somerset); SANDSTONE from Sussex; WEATHERED BOULDERS from the Craven Moors in Yorkshire; TUFA or TUFF (porous stone) from Moreton-in-the-Marsh, Gloucestershire. If one had the room to build such a rockery, and the money to buy the rock, one could do the same. For sandstone is excellent for many alpines that won't thrive on some kinds of limestone (often harmful to lime-hating plants such as Alpine Rhododendrons* and the exquisite sky-blue *Lithospermum diffusum*). Sussex sandstone is ideal for most plants, since it holds water.

Water-worn, weathered limestone, of which there are many kinds, the finest, most pleasing to the eye perhaps being that from Westmorland and north-west Yorkshire. Big, rectangular blocks give valuable scenic effects on sloping grassland: picturesque even without alpine plants to adorn them. It is all right to use them of course in gardens in or near Westmorland and Yorkshire; but only the very rich could afford to have the stone sent any great distance. Attractive limestone comes also from Purbeck and

---

* True, *Rhododendron ferrugineum* and R. *hirsutum* grow on limestone in the Swiss Alps, but only in pockets of fairly deep acid leaf soil (debris soil) washed down by the melting snows. And the plants are the surface-rooting kinds.

Cheddar and large blocks of it give a remarkable touch of mountain scenery to a garden.

Ragstone is indigenous to Kent and the adjacent counties. A fresh-water limestone, greyish-blue in colour, perhaps one of the hardest of the several different kinds, it is among the hardest of all rockery stones. And it is worth while to remember that the lime it contains normally remains insoluble and therefore harmless to lime-hating alpines grown on it or in association with it. This stone breaks irregularly owing to the large shells and fossil sponges present in it; I think it is seen at its best and most attractive when placed to give the effect of running strata in large rock gardens.

Granite, like ragstone, is not a popular rockery stone, being harsh-looking, a cold grey stone got in blocks of an enormous size. It polishes well and is valued for building.

Chalk, a soft limestone, is wholly unsuitable and gardeners don't use it.

Tufa (technically known as tuff: the O.E.D. gives: *Calcareous tufa* 'a porous or vesicular carbonate of lime—*vesicular*: with more or less spherical cavities—generally deposited near the sources of calcareous springs'); it is either a rock ejected from volcanoes or a precipitated limestone formed by the action of water. Tufa, usually greyish in colour, is a porous stone, often friable and easily penetrated by a sharp tool to form holes in which certain plants may be grown. A lot of it we get from Denbighshire in North Wales.

Oolite rock is similar: it is composed of small spherical granules, like the hard roe of a fish—it is also known as roe-stone.

Tufa is a popular stone for rock gardening these days; it may be and often is treated with a mixture of soil and water (of a thickish consistency) poured over it and left to dry. The mixture enters the holes, settles there and helps to provide nutriment for the plants grown on it; these may be seedlings or maturer plants, depending on the size of the holes. Or seeds may be sown. (Saxatile plants such as *Sedum, Saxifraga, Sempervivum* are much at home here.)

Some soft sandstones are similarly treated (often those that have been newly quarried), though a thickish manure water (old cow dung and rain water) is used instead of mud. Or sometimes rice water is painted on when cold; both aid the weathering process and both form a sticky surface, to which air-borne seeds and spores adhere and eventually form a lichen– or moss-like covering.

Building

One can always learn something fresh from a rock-garden expert. Camillo Luca comes from Sardinia where a lot of tufa rock is found.

It is cheap there (or you can collect what you want in some districts where it is very abundant); but it is expensive in England, the most expensive of all rockery stone, Camillo says. But it weighs light and you buy it by the ton and get plenty of it; so bulk for bulk you will find it as cheap as, say, heavy limestone or sandstone (a cubic yard of limestone weighs about a ton). Tufa varies in colour; the white is less attractive than the greyish-brown or yellowish-brown. White rock or stonework looks like a cemetery, says Camillo, and polluted air turns limestone white.

Choose the natural stone of the district, if there is any. In Dorset, Derbyshire, Gloucestershire, Yorkshire it is plentiful; but I don't know of any here in Bucks. You may have to get permission to remove the stone—I'm not sure about this. If you do it on your own, you can't take very much and not any very big pieces.

The best way is to get a local nursery to supply the stone. They will send well weathered stuff suitable for the type of rockery you want to build.

If yours is a small garden, ten to one the nursery will advise you to buy tufa. It is possible to grow lime-hating plants on tufa rock that contains magnesium. You may rest assured that your nursery will send you the right sort of stone and the information (if you want it) about how to arrange it on the site you choose.*

* C. C. Field Ltd. of Bodfari, Denbigh, quote TUFA at £2·50 a cwt. Powell Jones Ltd. of Worthing, Sussex, quote SUSSEX SANDSTONE—£4·88 a ton; WESTMORLAND WATERWORN—£3·00 a ton; MENDIP LIMESTONE—£4·75 a ton. And G. G. Renouf Ltd. of New Southgate, London, N.11, give both colour and approximate weight of the pieces: KENTISH RAGSTONE—Buff/Grey, in approx. ½ cwt to 1¼ cwt pieces—£7·50 a ton; MENDIP MOUNTAIN—Red/Grey, approx. ½ cwt to 2 cwt pieces—£10·00 a ton. Many other kinds of rockery stone are supplied.

I watched Camillo Luca one autumn day starting work on a new rock garden just outside Beaconsfield, Bucks. It is a good time to build, since the weather is still warm and planting can be done as the work proceeds, or it can be left till spring. If you leave it till then, the rocks will have settled, though normally there is little or no chance of their sinking unless the soil beneath has been very deeply dug. And deep digging isn't necessary. Except to remove perennial weeds such as Bindweed, Nettles and Ground-elder.

Weathered sandstone blocks measuring roughly 2 feet by 18 inches were used. It all came from a local nursery and was originally quarried out three years ago from beds in Sussex. 'Set it the right way up,' said Camillo, 'with the strata running horizontally. It holds a lot of water like all sandstones. And soft rocks—like this—', he kicked a piece, 'flake after being frosted, specially if you stand them the wrong way up. Vertically . . .'

Because this Sussex sandstone holds water, it is excellent for moisture-loving plants, though of course you must have the right sort of soil as well.

The biggest pieces were put at the bottom of the slope, on which the rockery was being built. At the top tufa was used. 'Tufa I get for nothing in Sardinia: here you pay £2·50 a hundredweight for it.'

One thing he didn't do—which I always do—was to sink the stone an inch or two into the soil. I invariably do this because there often is, after a severe frost, a risk of the stone moving forward on a hard, smooth slope, however gentle the slope might be. Sinking it to the depth of an inch is sufficient to prevent any such movement. On close-clipped or mown grass, it is nearly always done, the stone then having the appearance of outcropping stone. Some pieces have an uneven base and consequently cannot lie flush with the ground, the space between the stone and the grass shows immediately and the stone looks as if it had been dumped on the grass by accident. On bare ground, soil can if necessary be used to fill any spaces.

Dressed stone or building stone, bricks, brick-bats, clinkers and anything of that sort should never be used; far better to use

17

old stumps of trees,* partly burying them in the soil. Or steps can be cut in the soil, where there is a natural slope, and reinforced with strips of wood and stones; I have seen trailing alpine *Phlox* growing on steps made like this; and they can be planted in the middle, provided they are not allowed to creep too far. Another feature is the paved walk made of flags or of good quality cement slabs; in the interstices creeping alpine plants are grown. Those gardeners who are able to get quantities of this dressed stone gratis or for very little and use it should take care that the carved decorative parts are well hidden in the soil. In time the stone becomes covered with moss and lichen and consequently loses some of its harsh artificial look.

Rock-work, it has been said, makes a garden look cool; true, large rocks throw pleasing shadows on grass in mid-summer, but flat-topped ones in exposed places get very hot and may then be harmful to the plants growing on them, these perhaps being cushion varieties, and the rock, flat-topped tufa. 'Don't sprinkle them with water,' says Camillo, 'or you will boil them. Plant a tree to throw shade during the hottest part of the day.'

The important thing to do is to choose the correct site. A position facing west is better than one facing due south, unless there are trees or a hedge or a screen of some sort to afford the necessary shade. One facing north is all right for shade-loving alpines but might prove too cold for some when they are in bloom early in the year.

A scorched-up rock garden is an ugly sight; it is perhaps inevitable if only a due-south aspect is available; the solution of course would be to plant the rockery made there with sun-loving desert plants, many of which would be annuals and suitable shrubs or shrublets such as *Cistus* (Rock-roses) and forget all about genuine alpines, the vast majority of which flourish only in semi-shady, rather moist places. Or simply plant winter-flowering bulbs—*Crocus imperati*; *C. sieberi*: lovely purples—and very early blooming things. 'Oh for the mountain mists to descend occasion-

---

* The *rootery* was a feature of some gardens at the end of the last century. The O.E.D's definition: 'A pile formed of tree-roots with interspersed soil for the ornamental growing of garden-plants.'

ally!' said Camillo after a drought of five weeks at the Beacons-field site. 'You should not have to water alpines.'

A due-east aspect is bad; and cold coupled with drought is fatal to most plants.

Trees provide shade but they must be at a distance and not near enough to overhang the rocks; for drippings from the branches, even the scantiest, will damage the plants underneath.

A background of some sort, say, of evergreens is useful, serving both as a screen against north-east winds and to show up the plants when in bloom to best advantage. Care must be taken to prevent any roots from invading and impoverishing the soil where the plants are growing. Very deep roots won't do much harm, but the surface roots you discover when you are digging over the site, which, by the way, must be perfectly drained, must be cut off and new ones prevented from spreading by sinking corrugated iron in front of the hedge to arrest their growth.

Should or shouldn't a rockery be visible from the house? Most designers say, No.

It depends on the size of the garden. In a large garden the rockery, like other quasi-natural or 'free' features, is usually relegated to the wild part, where perhaps a water-garden—which may be an artificial stream running through rocks—is situated. Normally paths and a drive lead to and from a house and lawns surround it or best part of it. A shrubbery bounding one side of the lawn is as a rule visible from the house and perhaps some windows look out on to flower-borders and beds. They are attractive to the eye and easily seen.

A rockery often displays only its rocks till one goes closer and walks through it and makes a closer examination, many of the plants growing in sheltered pockets among the rocks. This is not always so of course and a rockery can be near the house and yet not at all visible; for it may be hidden by a wall or by a hedge. Rockery-banks and wall-gardens—retaining walls—are often built close to the house for the simple reason that the soil bank happens to be situated close to the house or adjacent to it; but they are not classed as genuine rockeries, any more than is an alpine lawn, or crazy-paving, in which alpines are grown.

In the small garden at Beaconsfield a screen of hybrid ever-green Rhododendrons concealed the rockery and none of it was visible from any of the windows. In the small modern garden—often less than half an acre—it is perhaps difficult to conceal any feature completely; but it is usually possible to hide smallish rocks by the judicious placing of shrubs or shrub-like plants: bamboos are useful, provided you can control them in some way, for most of them spread much farther than you want them to.

As regards the actual lay-out of the rockery, this will depend on the site, its contours and the like, and of course on the designer's preferences and on his experience in the art and science of construction. So on one site you could have a number of differently-designed rock-gardens and all could be good.

Camillo's was a miniature, with a tiny moraine or scree made in a pocket at the back of a big rock and a very miniature alpine lawn at the base, running round the sunny side of the rocks.

At the top were the tufa rocks, the largest about 10 inches wide and high, firmly held in position by the soil; holes were bored in the tops of some to hold suitable plants. Larger rocks, some tufa, some Sussex sandstone, were placed half-way down the slope, and the biggest, about 2 feet long, were at the bottom. These were too heavy for one man to move easily and were therefore put in place by the nurserymen who delivered them to the site. This is a point worth remembering, especially by those who have to build a rockery single-handed. Camillo's comment was brief: 'Don't strain your guts.' You can leave the rocks, as he did, for a few weeks before planting. Stand back and view your work: it may give you some ideas on what to plant and how to set out the plants.

The most unsatisfactory type of rockery is that too often seen unfortunately in small gardens and that defined by dictionaries as 'an artificial mound or bank of stones with rock-plants etc. planted in the interstices . . .' The 'mound' is the great defect; the 'bank of stones' would be all right, provided it were a natural bank, that is to say, there were two planes or levels of soil, one separated from the other by a bank; but 'mound' implies an artificial piling up of stones above the natural surface and has nothing to recommend it. It also implies a mound of soil on which and in which the rocks are to be set and from which, obviously, all moisture soon drains away.

Rockeries are best built in a depression or an artificial dell or hollow; but should never be mound-like—up one side and down the other. It often means that you will have to excavate a depression or hollow; it can be roughly saucer-shaped or more elongated; and the soil removed, if on the light, sandy side, may be used to fill up spaces between the stones or rocks when they are being set in position; if it is clay, it is useless and the foundation must be thoroughly dug over and well drained. A pathway through the dell is the most simple method of settling the design. Use flattish stones of good quality and let the pathway bend slightly to the right or to the left; it will descend a little toward the middle and then rise again to the opposite side. The sides will slope naturally down to the path and the deepest parts will be in the middle. The arrangement and disposition of the rocks must be left to the builder of the rock-garden; the largest rocks should be set at the lowest part; but no precise outlining of the hollow should be attempted; one or two of the largest rocks should be sunk both at the entrance and the exit for instance.

Soil

Most of the rock plants we grow thrive in ordinary garden soil. We can name half a dozen—that come easily to mind—and find that they all do well in the soil we get from a kitchen-garden that is under general cultivation: *Arabis, Aubrietia* (common kinds); *Armeria* (the common Thrift); *Campanula portenschlagiana*, the bluish-mauve, mat-forming Bellflower that blooms in early summer; *Dianthus* (pink Rock-pinks); alpine *Phlox*. You could cover a small rockery with these, which of course you don't want to do—superior quality rocks are always good to look at unadorned—and these plants need no special kinds of soil.

If the soil happens to be a heavy clay, it should be removed and replaced by loam. On the whole I have found that a sandy soil, a lightish soil, is better than any rich, garden loam. The foundation clay of a site cannot be removed entirely, so it must be lightened by the addition of ashes or crushed cinders, sand and sifted leafmould or powdered peat. This treatment holds good too for large quantities of clay you find in parts of a large rockery when you are preparing good-sized pockets for certain plants.

Mix your own soil in a barrow and keep what you don't use in a box for later mulching and replenishing. Use two bucketfuls of sifted loam, not recently manured, two parts of sifted peat or leafmould and one bucket of sharp sand.* Mix these ingredients well together and add—instead of manure, which must not be used—a 5-inch flower-potful of bonemeal. This compost is suitable for any of the so-called easy plants that are grown in the average rock-garden; it is reasonably moisture retentive.

Some alpines however prosper only in thin, almost starved ground; and this must be remembered when making a selection. Certain species of *Genista* and *Cytisus* and most of the *Cistus* need poor soil, though it is usually better to start them off in a little of the compost described above; afterwards no top-dressings or mulchings will be necessary. (For *Arabis* and *Aubrietia*, the latter especially, a mulch of sifted leafmould is recommended: applied after the flowers have faded and the plants have been pruned.)

Some of the *Genista* and *Cytisus* (Brooms), with their trailing stems, are well adapted to growing on rock-work. They like full sun and hot places and are not as a rule very long lived. The best way to grow the different species of dwarf trailing Brooms is to sow seeds in the crevices where you want the plants to grow and bloom. Sow the seed in equal parts of sand and soil.

Cistus (Rock-roses) are probably overlarge for most rockeries, but they might serve as a background, planted, for example, at the top, as Camillo had planted evergreen hybrid Rhododendrons as a screen.

The soil for alpine Rhododendrons and other ericaceous things, such as Heathers (*Erica*), must be lime free, and deep and rich in vegetable matter. You might find that some of the plants mentioned above grow all right in an acid medium, but they will make a lot of leafy, sappy growth at the expense of flowers, and will eventually deteriorate.

Don't however plant any Rhododendrons or the so-called

* It must be sharp sand: builders' yellow sand is too fine. Coarse gritty 'Bedfordshire Crystals' is excellent and obtainable from many stone distributors.

Azaleas in pure leaf-mould or peat, since growing in this medium for a season or two will cause them to damp off and rot. In their natural habitats many grow in almost pure sand and prosper well. The bushy *Rhododendron mucronulatum* from Korea, a most valuable species that blooms during an open winter at Christmas, is one of these and suitable as a background shrub. In a large rockery it may be grown among the rocks and will benefit much from the shelter they afford.

Thin sandy soils are easy enough to provide; an acid soil might prove more difficult, especially if you collect your own sort in neighbouring woods where there might be a chalk sub-soil. If you come to sand where you dig, you needn't worry; but if you strike chalk, it would be worth your while to have the leafmould you collect tested for acid and alkaline ratios. Many nurseries who specialize in soil products have a scientific department who will undertake the job. You can of course buy genuine sphagnum moss peat which many firms advertise as, 'Dry, perfectly granulated (chopped or powdered), sterile, weed and pest free . . .' A good buy for gardeners who intend growing some of the expensive alpine Rhododendrons.*

No doubt atmospheric moisture in the shape of mountain mists helps considerably to sustain these creeping shrubs and keep them in a healthy, flourishing condition. We certainly find it difficult to grow many of them even in specially-prepared pockets of peaty soil. R. *hirsutum* (mentioned on page 9), from the Alps of Central Europe, is found on pure limestone but well rooted in vegetable detritus matter deposited by rain or by water trickling down from the higher slopes. This species is said to be tolerant of lime in garden soil, but I doubt very much whether this is so. Unless your soil is genuinely acid, don't grow it. Anyhow, it seldom gives much of a show in cultivation. The hybrid creeping kinds are usually more successful and seem to be more popular than the species. R. × 'Elizabeth', a cross between R. *griersonianum* and a form of R. *forrestii*, is exceptionally hardy

---

* Some of these cost £1·50 a plant or more. R. *repens* and R. *forrestii* are two. They are natives of mountainous regions in China and Tibet; in some places R. *forrestii*, with its lovely scarlet-crimson narrow bells, grows 4 or 5 feet up the face of moist rocks.

and tough and is often seen growing well and covered with blood-red flowers in the rock-garden. These Rhododendrons, both hybrids and species, are very useful plants to grow since they are evergreen and their leaves are attractive all through the year. They bloom in our gardens unfortunately when the majority of alpines are in bloom; but in nature the flowering period of the species depends on the altitude: in the Alps R. *ferrugineum* and R. *hirsutum* exposed to the tumults of the highest snowy regions are found blooming as late as August and September.

The extreme opposite of these creeping shrubs are the desert plants of the tropics, many of which grow in sand and collect their nutrition from torrential rains and store it in their fleshy stems and leaves. The problem here is not soil, but temperature. We might get it hot enough, despite the vagaries of our summer weather, but we can seldom keep these desert rock-plants alive through a cold, damp winter. They are often best treated as annuals or lifted in the autumn and housed indoors. The *Gazania* from South Africa, with spreading stems and showy orange-coloured daisy-like flowers, are magnificent rockery plants but suitable only for the very warmest places in Britain.

Moist soil, kept practically wet by running water, is necessary for certain rock-Primulas and Marsh Marigolds (*Caltha palustris*). The double flowered one *Var. plena*, blooming in April, is a gem for a rockery built near a stream or a ditch or an artificial pool. These wet soils however must not be stagnant but well drained.

And very gritty, moist soil is necessary for the creeping, moss-like alpine *Arenaria balearica* which, when once it gets established on a cool, shady rock—one facing due north—, quickly covers it and overruns everything else growing near. It has been called a soil-less plant, but of course you get well-rooted specimens in pots from the nurseries. It flourishes on tufa and is ideally planted by sowing seed in a cavity.

Moraine or scree soil is dealt with more fully in Chapter 4. Suffice it to say that the miniature moraine, which in gardening is the same as the scree, is made for those alpines that live in the debris of glacier formations; it consists of loose, broken stony materials, through which snow water from the mountainside trickles and percolates, bringing leafy, vegetable matter and

24

various kinds of soil and detritus along with it. It is in these media that the scree plants grow and prosper. Not so easy in a rock-garden. It will be necessary to have a deep layer of drainage material, say, of broken rock and stones; the scree soil required will be mixed with this and during long spells of dry weather it will be necessary to use the watering-can; though in the small modern garden a continual supply of water can easily be had by using a hose.

Choice of Plants

The problem of choice of plants is most easily solved, some gardeners say, by studying a catalogue. True you get a brief description of the plants that helps you perhaps to decide where to grow them; and less often you are given the time of the year when they bloom or when they are at their best. More important, I think, is it to see the plants growing preferably at a botanic garden, where they have been chosen and planted and tended by experts. And, if possible, to see them both in flower and before they bloom and in a quiescent state, when they look very different, the evergreen ones often having attractive foliage in winter.

Camillo visited Kew once a month for a year, studying the alpines in the rock-garden, noting those that were in bloom and the length of time they bloomed. Nothing, he thought, lasted very long, never more than a week or two. This is true of some plants; but there are many that have a long succession of flowers, the individual blooms lasting only a week or so; some, such as the Rock-roses, only a day; but the actual flowering period continues for a month or more. It's a fascinating thing to plan the planting of a rock-garden. One should aim at having something in bloom all through the year; but the smaller the rock-garden, the more difficult that is to achieve, of course.

The type of rockery and the kind of rocks used will obviously influence our choice. For example, a rockery built in an open sunny spot and consequently having little or no shade on it all day, will require different plants from that which is built in a shady place. Furthermore, the large rockery, with its huge sandstone blocks, will be able to accommodate plenty of large plants and show them off to perfection. Smaller rocks and you need smaller plants.

For my part I like to have a number of winter-blooming alpines in all types of rockeries. One that comes to mind is *Iris unguicularis*, which, according to botanists, blooms from November to March. In my garden in South Bucks., it blooms from February to the end of April. It is what we might call a rock-face type of plant. That is to say, it needs a position, partly to protect it, at the base of a bluff-like rock, vertical but not overhanging. Strange to say, this mid-winter plant is the most fragile-looking of all our garden Irises; the flowers are a delicate lavender, slightly fragrant and spring up out of a mass of rush-like leaves. There is a dwarf variety called *cretensis*—mauve flowers veined with violet—that is suitable for small rockeries. (A fuller description of this species is given in Chapter 3, page 70.)

Several other rhizomatous and bulbous plants are ideally suited to a rock-face position. They are often on the tender side and bloom in autumn when the weather is getting cooler or in mid-winter; the background of rock helps to preserve the flowers during a hard frost.

Nerine filifolia is the species usually chosen for growing against a rock, since it is the dwarfest, about 12 inches high. It is not so hardy as *N. Bowdenii*, from 18 to 24 inches high, which is too tall for the average small rockery. In *N. filifolia* the clusters or lily-like flowers (8 to 10) are rose-red and bloom about October, depending on the district. Camillo thinks it is suitable only for the alpine house and for people who can afford to renew it, if grown outside. The leaves are slender and 8 inches long, rather like those of the winter Iris. Nerines are natives of South Africa. *N. sarniensis*, one of the loveliest, though tender, is known as the Guernsey Lily.

Schizostylis coccinea, the Kaffir Lily, also from South Africa, is a rhizomatous plant that is occasionally grown in large rockeries where there are vertical rocks 3 feet or more high. The flowers, scarlet, come in a spike, like those of a miniature Gladiolus, and bloom in October and November when little else is in bloom. Then the plants give a fine show of flowers against vertical rocks facing due south where they get all the sun possible. The only other place where these plants can be grown outside is at the foot of a south wall.

Completely different in style are the Miniature Roses that are derived from the species *Rosa chinensis minima*, known as the Fairy Rose. There are many charming garden forms available and all like a sunny position. At the foot of a south-facing rock they certainly get it and will start blooming in May and continue intermittently through to the early autumn. They are often regarded critically by gardeners, who state that they are not suitable for rock-work, that they are too formal in appearance, too exact as it were. But one in isolation, against a rock-face, looks all right, I think. The important thing to remember when planting the little bush is not to set the roots too near the rock, for the plant needs room to spread out its branches. The average height of these miniature roses is 12 inches. Two charming varieties are 'Midget', bright crimson, striped with white; and 'Pumila', with single deep pink flowers measuring an inch across. There are several that grow to a height of only 6 inches; my favourite is 'Perla Rosa' that has rose-pink flowers, with a paler centre, a perfect miniature rose-bush (6 inches) for the miniature rock-garden. The rock against which it is planted need not be more than 9 inches high.

For growing against vertical rocks facing due north or for those that get plenty of shade on them you need moisture-loving plants such as the Primulas. *Primula denticulata*, which comes from the Himalayas, has roundish heads of light mauve flowers borne on 10-inch stems that spring up out of rosettes of ovalish pale green leaves. As with the miniature roses, the ball of roots should not be set too near the base of the rock. This plant is easily raised from seed, as are most Primulas, Polyanthuses and Primroses. They may be sown in sandy leafy soil where they are to bloom, though as they take a very long time to germinate, it is wise to mark the place with an upturned glass jar or cloche. All these plants will throw seedlings *in situ*. So you will seldom be without.

The common Primrose is an ideal plant for a position at the base of a shady rock. *Primula rosea* is another but does best in moist, even wet, soil. However, you can get it to flourish in open gritty leaf-soil in shade and it throws plenty of seed and increases in that way. It won't succeed in a crevice higher up in a rockery unless the soil in which it grows can be kept permanently moist: this is possible of course if there is water dripping down the rocks from an artificial cascade.

The sheer perpendicular rock or bluff-face has of course no crevices; but they will be found practically everywhere else in a rockery. Crevices, cavities, fissures are the places where alpines grow and, given the right soil, will thrive and increase, the seedlings often springing up where they are not wanted. A plant to watch in this respect is *Meconopsis cambrica*, the Welsh Poppy that throws seedlings all over the garden. It likes a semi-shady crevice, but it would be wise not to grow it in a small rockery. When the brilliant orange flowers are massed, the effect is startling as it is in the gardens at Windsor Castle, where the plant grows in hundreds on high rocks. 'You'd be crazy to grow it in a small rockery,' a gardener once told me. 'In a couple of years you wouldn't be able to see the rocks.' Pulling up clumps of it regularly, helps to weaken it.

The spreading mat-like Campanulas are much less invasive and they don't throw seedlings all over the rockery. And actually many of them are better in a pocket made up on a rock tilting slightly backward, with another behind it. Embedded in a gentle slope—as they should be—the rocks will have plenty of soil around them. Species such as *C. portenschlagiana* (and its varieties) with small mauvish bells, make thick mats of flowers in a pocket, in either sun or shade.

Small rooted pieces may be planted in crevices on a vertical part of a rock-garden, or on a rockery wall, and they will then form a sheet of flowers and give the impression of a trailing plant. *C. cochlearifolia*, sometimes listed in catalogues under *C. pusilla*, produces a mass of underground stems and should be planted only where you want it to run freely.

Lewisia are occasionally grown in sunny crevices but need protection from the winter wet and damp that so quickly rot the crowns of the plants. Panes of glass are usually placed over them from November onward. The soil must be limefree; the position sunny. *Lewisia Howelli* forms flat, wide rosettes of green leaves, from which arise the stems, bearing clusters of deep rose-pink

28

flowers; it blooms in summer. There are other species as lovely but all difficult plants in the average rockery. Most people grow them in the alpine house.

Sedums like crevices; and there are varieties suitable for sunny or for shady places. Saxifrages too; many of these are cushion plants and should be grown in holes made in tufa rock. (See Chapters 2 and 3 where full descriptions of the plants are given.)

The alpine kinds of Rhododendrons do well at the base of a cool rock facing west or in a pocket with the same aspect. They like partial shade and of course a completely limefree soil. You won't get them to climb up the rock face in a garden but they will spread out and make evergreen mats of flowers, some of the Azalea type being covered in blossom that completely hides the leaves.

For cool, moist, shady crevices on the north side of a rockery *Ramonda* (Pyrenean Primroses) are the plants to grow. They need moisture—almost wet places—all through the growing season and therefore may occasionally want a good soaking with a watering-can in summer. And rain water when you can get it. The soil must be peaty and lime free. The leaves come in a rosette and are wrinkled and hairy; the flowers, usually mauve, like big Potato Flowers, are borne on 6-inch stems. *Ramonda myconi var. rosea* is the finest; the flowers are a deep rose colour; there is a white form—*alba*; and the type is purple. Most gardeners prefer to grow *Ramonda* in pots in the alpine house.

Campanulas when planted one above the other in the crevices of a rock-wall give one the impression of trailing plants, as I've already said; but the genuine trailer has long stems that form a mat-like mass of foliage and flowers that can be lifted up with one's hand like a piece of material. The rocks used for these plants are best placed horizontally on top of one another: pieces about 9 inches thick and 18 inches long, giving in the aggregate a height of about 2 feet which is high enough to show off the character and beauty of the plants. The rocks must slant backward slightly into the soil behind.

Arabis and *Aubrietia* are two of the most popular trailing plants and seen in practically every garden. Both like a sunny position, though they will flower freely in partial shade. The Soapwort

Saponaria ocymoides, with masses of tiny bright pink flowers covering it and hiding the leaves, makes a sheet of colour on vertical rocks in early summer.

In shady places you can grow *Arenaria montana*, for it likes a certain amount of shade on its large round white flowers. (The species *A. balearica* is a creeping plant with minute white flowers and thrives only in deep shade.) For high rocks facing west plant *Clematis alpina*, with violet-blue flowers and let it trail down the front; its long hanging stems and flowers will form a sheet of colour in late April. And for mid-winter plant in the same position, or in one facing north, the yellow winter-blooming Jasmine, *Jasminum nudiflorum*; it will prosper well in any shady part of a rock garden.

The larger the plant, the farther back on the wall it should be planted; both the Clematis and the Jasmine need setting at least a foot away from the rock, in deep soil, and the stems trained forward and down the rock-face.

Another class of alpines is the creeping, mat-forming kind such as *Arenaria balearica*, mentioned above; it has light green moss-like foliage and minute white star-like flowers about the size of a pin's head. The New Zealand *Raoulia lutescens* makes a greyish close carpet, almost resembling lichen on a stone or the bark of a tree, and is most decorative on a flat rock at any time of the year. Another carpeter is the foliage thyme, *Thymus pseudolanuginosus*, with grey-green woolly fragrant leaves. It has a delightful, silky look and likes a sunny rock to grow on; it can be grown in any position in the rockery and is often used in the alpine lawn.

The great beauty of these tight, close-creeping plants is that they emphasize the contours of the rock over which they grow and so colour it with grey, green or a silver sheen, like patches of lichen or moss on lovely ageing stone.

Care of the Plants

'Don't grow everything you set your heart on' is a maxim for every gardener planning a rockery. We visit the Chelsea Flower Show and find all the alpines there that we long to grow. A drift of brilliant blue Gentians. A wide sweep of alpine Rhododendrons. Many rare tender plants from the high Andes. And all miraculously in bloom for the opening day. Most of them, however, perhaps all of them, are grown in pots and sunk carefully into the soil. And many have been either forced in greenhouses or held back perhaps by prolonged refrigeration till they are wanted. It is wise to ask first before placing an order what sort of soil an alpine wants. You will be told that the Gentians do well in an ordinary loam; but that the Rhododendrons must have a special acid, limefree foil on the moist side. So have your soil tested before you pay £1·50 for the one you want. Now you can use the substance called 'Sequestrine' to make your soil permanently suitable for those ericaceous plants. This substance, in powder form, is used for correcting lime-induced iron deficiency (chlorosis) in soils. It enables lime-hating plants to be grown in chalky or calcareous soils; it is also an excellent stimulant to Heathers, Gentians and many other rather difficult rock plants.*

Top dressing, with powdered peat or leafmould (half-decayed oak leaves are particularly rich in nutrition), is necessary once a year and best applied in April after a heavy rain. Use a good layer, say, 4 inches deep; a sprinkling is practically useless. And ordinary plants such as *Arabis, Aubrietia, Dianthus* and the like benefit enormously from a yearly mulching. Use peat or leafmould mixed with the same quantity of fine sand. See that the soil is well moistened by rain or by watering before you apply the mulch.

As regards actual organic manure, fresh dung is never used or wanted; but a very little old rotted cow dung which powders easily in the fingers may be added to the leafmould and applied in spring, though not all plants need it. Do not give any sort of organic manure to any plant during autumn or winter, since it keeps the ground cold and wet and will often kill the plant.

A little very weak liquid manure may be given to some plants coming into bloom, such as the hybrid alpine Rhododendrons; use it only after a shower or when the soil is damp. Heathers (*Erica*) don't require it; they do best in cultivation in rather thin sandy soils. A starvation diet is best perhaps—it is for many Heathers.

* Add a little 'Sequestrine' to your tap water when watering Rhododendrons.

The best time for planting is September; I choose this month because the soil still retains some of its summer warmth and roots find their way around more easily in warm soils. Spring—late spring—is good, though the soil may not always be fit then; and you will need to water your plants regularly through the summer months. September is usually followed by cool moist weather that is more propitious and healthy for all growing things.

Because, however, plants are nowadays raised in pots and sent out from the nurseries in pots, planting is done practically at any time; you can set out your plants in the garden the day they arrive (perhaps mid-August) and have them immediately in bloom. But they need watching and carefully tending, watering and perhaps shading from the hot scorching sun. In fact, my rule is to nurse all plants, rock, shrub, perennials, for three years before finally releasing them to look after themselves. By the end of the third year they should be firmly established; if they are not going to succeed, they will probably have died before then.

Right soil and situation and right feeding—which is manuring—are of paramount importance in plant culture. If you choose the right place for your plant, sunny or shady, as the case may be, you will never be confronted with the difficult task of shifting them. Be sure then that you decide on the right place, especially if the plants happen to be shrubs like Brooms and Cistus with long, fine roots; both these seldom survive a move. Rhododendrons, on the other hand, are much safer; they make a strong ball of roots and can be moved years after planting them.

There are unfortunately some plants that are almost impossible to get rid of once they are established. One of these is the well known 'Snow-in-Summer', *Cerastium tomentosum*. This, with its whitish, silvery foliage—whiter on poor, starved soils—is lovely as a foliage rock plant; but it is an insidious creeper, sending out masses of underground stems everywhere. Like the orange Welsh Poppy, *Meconopsis cambrica* (page 28), it soon covers a small rockery and smothers everything else in it; it might take years of pulling up the runners to get rid of the plant—its counterpart in the world of weeds is the notorious Ground Elder (*Aegopodium podagraria*). Other plants are invasive but not so strong as the *Cerastium*. The most suitable place for this creeper-trailer is a hot

Gentian acaulis, the popular, though difficult, spring Gentian; described on page 65.

A little grey foliage plant with yellow daisy flowers (*Euryops acraeus*); it needs a sunny well-drained position.

Gypsophila repens var. rosea: an ideal plant for a paved walk; see page 164.

sunny bank where nothing else is to be planted. In any rockery it is useless and quickly becomes a nuisance.

Most rock plants may be pruned back when their flowers have finished blooming. The stems of genuine trailers often get too long for the place the plants occupy. *Arabis* and *Aubrietia* are inclined to ramp after a year or two. Double *Arabis* resents drastic pruning and need not be touched at all for some years; or it should be pruned leniently. *Aubrietia,* on the other hand, can be cut right back and will start sprouting again in early autumn.

Some rock shrubs such as *Genista* and most Brooms are best just tipped to remove the dead flowers. The faded flowers should be removed from Rhododendrons before they set seed. This advice is always given by raisers of these shrubs and its importance is emphasized by them. This is an easy job in the rock garden, where the shrubs are small and low-growing, but presents more difficulties when they are tall, say, 20-foot mature plants, such as one sees in big shrubberies.

Alpines such as the mat-forming Gentians and Campanulas, growing in pockets, simply need dividing up when the clumps get too large and look as if they are going to spill over the sides. The best time for dividing clumps of spring-blooming alpines is September; for autumn flowerers April. Some plants resent root disturbance, however—some Gentians do—methods of treating these are described along with the plants in later chapters.

Propagation

There are several ways of increasing our stocks of plants. Sowing seeds, taking cuttings, layering and division, are preferred by most amateurs. These are comparatively straightforward methods. Division and offsets, such as bulbils, are the easiest and quickest; sowing seeds and layering, the slowest.

The actual sowing of seeds is simple enough of course: one collects it from the plant, sprinkles it thinly on a suitable soil or compost and covers it either with sand or a fine, sifted, leafy loam. Seed may be sown in pots indoors in autumn and winter or outside from April onward. Some seeds germinate quickly: in a few weeks: often that which is collected fresh, while the pods are still green but nicely swollen; some lie dormant for a year or more and the seeds of most alpines benefit from being frozen and lying under snow through the winter months. After that period they germinate freely, appearing like thickly-sown mustard-and-cress.

Often the seedlings thrown vary considerably from the parent plants; this is nearly always the case with hybrids: species are more reliable. Many gardeners prefer to get their seeds from a reputable seedsman; they are reasonably cheap, there is always a wide range to choose from, and furthermore the information given is most helpful. *Gentiana acaulis** costs 5p a packet and one firm advises: 'Sow in pots or pans filled with light, porous soil and give perfect drainage. Sink in ashes outdoors, protecting from sun and heavy rain, and expose to frost and snow in winter. Move to greenhouse or frame in spring.' You can get species of *Arabis, Campanula, Dianthus, Maconopsis* and varieties of *Aubrietia* and hybrid Rhododendrons and Azaleas. In fact enough plants to stock a small rockery, I suppose, for under a pound.

Division as a means of propagation is simple: you need a healthy, well established plant that you dig up, and from it pull off sizeable pieces with roots; and these are re-planted to form new plants. The strongest and most healthy parts are on the outside of the parent plant. Nothing could be easier and quicker. September is the ideal month for this work. Small alpines are easily pulled to pieces with the aid of one's fingers. Often you can get what you want from a plant without disturbing it much: you needn't dig it up: you simply tear pieces off with an old table-fork.

Alpines with fibrous roots that spread and form thick mat-like growths or tufts are the usual type we choose for this method of propagation. Some of the Gentians are good examples: for instance, *Gentiana acaulis* (spring); and *G. sino-ornata* (autumn). Division is best done immediately after the flowering period. Primulas are easily divided and benefit too from this treatment after a year or two. *Primula juliae*, with deep velvety purple primrose-like flowers in January, is a fine mat-forming species that is very easily divided, a single spreading clump making a dozen or more new plants.

* Now listed as *G. excisa* in most catalogues.

Sempervivums (House Leeks) form spreading mats of leaf-rosettes, and are easily propagated by pulling off the side-shoots or offsets. These quickly root in sandy loam.

Many other plants can be increased in this way: various kinds of Saxifrages, for instance. I divide all those of the Mossy Section; 'London Pride' (*Saxifraga umbrosa*); most of the stronger growing Kabschia kinds such as *S. x apiculalra*, a wide-spreading mat-plant; and many of the Silver (Encrusted) Saxifrages.

Cuttings are quicker than seeds—about six months to form new plants—but slower than division. We usually choose half-ripened pieces of wood (or stem) of the plants, set them in sandy soil in a shady part of the garden and cover them with a bell-glass or a cloche.

Cuttings are taken in late summer, usually when the plants have finished blooming, and unflowered pieces pulled off with a heel—a portion of the parent stem attached—are necessary. They should be short, not more than about 2 inches long, the lower leaves removed, and the pieces then inserted in damp, sandy soil to a third of their length. I leave cuttings of most Alpines— *Arabis, Aubrietia, Dianthus, Phlox* and the like—for six months, covered tightly with a bell-glass, and plant them out (or the new plants thus formed) in their permanent places in spring; I never shift them in winter and bring them indoors, for I find that I often lose a lot when I do this. Alpine cuttings don't mind the cold.

Cuttings of Heathers (*Erica*) may, however, be struck indoors, under a bell-glass well shaded from the sun. Use pieces an inch long; insert them in damp sand and leave them till you see they are burgeoning, the tiny new shoots appearing at the tops.

Nowadays most gardeners use one of the proprietary rooting preparations; one, called Hormone Rooting Powder, is easily applied and usually mixed with the soil, or the bottom of the cutting is dipped in the powder or the solution and then inserted in the rooting medium.

Layering is practised by many gardeners who have plants with suitable low hanging branches; often these branches which reach the ground throw out strong roots at the point where they touch the soil.

Alpine Rhododendrons are frequently layered. Make a nick in the under part of the hanging branch, bring the branch down into the soil; cover it with a sandy leafy rooting medium—two parts of silver sand to one part of finely-sifted leafmould—and peg it firmly in position. Layering takes a long time; leave the layered branches for at least a year.

Dianthus are often layered, their long, jointed stems lending themselves well to this kind of propagation. They take about six months to form roots. The best time for layering plants is spring.

Pests and Diseases that Attack Rockery Plants

It has been said that plants growing in the garden, if they are being correctly cultivated, seldom if ever suffer from diseases. It is those grown in pots indoors that are more liable to attack. This is probably true, since artificial environment, artificial atmosphere, often induce unnatural growth which is prone to parasitic diseases: Bacteria, Fungi, Viruses, etc.—or to Functional disorders. In the garden of course we are often up against damage done by birds, ants, mice, dogs, cats and rabbits. We can keep these at bay, or most of them: nowadays we get practically every sort of aid we want from the chemist and the seedsman. An insecticide called Py-Spray Concentrate is described as '... effective against Black Fly, Green Fly, Thrips, Weevils, Sawfly, Caterpillars, Ants and many other insects ...' There are Pepper Powders to keep off cats and dogs, and an evil-smelling substance to defeat rabbits; though it may be necessary to put strong wire-netting round all shrubs that rabbits go for—I use both the evil-smelling stuff and wire-netting and a shot-gun.

Birds are beautiful and their song an enchantment. But how can we keep them off the garden? We can rig up bird scarers, though they are unsightly and nobody likes them. The best way is to arrange black cotton criss-crossed on twigs above the plants that are most often attacked. The important thing obviously is to watch and see which plants they go for. Common rock plants such as *Arabis* and *Aubrietia* are never touched in my garden; but Polyanthuses are pulled to pieces. Except those planted near the house—right up against a north window—and those that grow under trees. Black cotton is probably the answer.

Other pests are more easily checked and ultimately destroyed: there are insecticides for slugs and snails and caterpillars, and a 'mouse powder' that seems to help in dry weather, though traps often have to be used. But watch your pets. And so far I've never heard of a bird being caught in a mouse-trap; but it could be.

Slugs, snails, caterpillars attack some of our loveliest rock plants. A gardener friend says, 'Just pick 'em off when you see them. But you've got to keep at it . . . I never use them poison powders in my garden . . .' But most of us do nowadays, for we haven't time to go round picking off pests one at a time.

Functional diseases are usually at a minimum when rockery plants are growing as they should be. Strong, healthy, vigorous alpines, well established have obviously been planted in the right place and in the right soil. Long periods of drought often do harm as do long periods of hard biting frost, but healthy, well established plants soon recover.

CHAPTER 2

Take Your Choice

Not many true alpine plants are grown in our rockeries. But
hundreds of other plants are available and suitable for the purpose;
many are found wild in places far removed from mountains.
Some, such as *Cistus* (shrubby rock-roses), are natives of the hot
Mediterranean regions, where they are often found growing on
rock-like promontories or on dry scorching slopes. But they do
not grow in mountainous places at high altitudes.

In the European Alps the lowest altitude at which true alpines
grow and flourish lies between 5,000 and 7,000 feet above sea-
level. Because it is impossible to reproduce the climatic and
weather conditions prevalent in high mountain country, it is
extremely difficult to get these plants to grow successfully for
very long in our rock-gardens. Are they worth all the trouble?
Not really, unless you are a collector. And collectors usually have
properly constructed alpine houses where temperature, atmospheric conditions, amount of light, can be controlled to a certain
extent, so that the plants have a better chance of surviving. For
the collector it is a triumph to get these plants to flower and
thrive. There are alpines that grow at sea-level in snowy arctic
regions and some at an altitude of three or four thousand feet in
warmer parts of the world. According to botanists there are
about sixty genuine alpine families (genera); and close on six
hundred others containing plants suitable for growing in rockeries. Sub-alpines, many of them (plants growing near the snow-
line); many are shrublets that creep along the ground; there are
dwarf flowers like the Sardinian Iris (*Iris Chamaeiris*)* and all the
tiny spring bulbs.

* This Iris is excellent for massing along the top of a low retaining wall (see
page 108).

Most rock-garden enthusiasts nowadays, although often attracted by a rare difficult plant, grow those that need the minimum amount of care and attention. There are hundreds to choose from, many being very easy to grow.

Various kinds are described in the following pages. More space is given to those plants that should be grown in pockets, crevices, fissures or against a rock face. Trailers, ideally suited to a wall-garden, are more fully described in Chapter 30, pages 94–120.

A

Acaena microphylla (the specific epithet *microphylla* means small-leaved), one of the so-called New Zealand Burrs—not all the *Acaena* are natives of that country: some come from South America and other tropical parts—this is regarded as the choicest for the rockery. It is one of the creeping, mat-like plants so useful for covering rocks (like the *Raoulia, Arenaria* and *Thymus* mentioned in the previous chapter, page 30. Our plant has tiny, rose-like evergreen leaves composed of minute leaflets about ¼ inch long that vary in colour from bluish-grey to bronze; the spreading dense foliage forming a mat about 1 inch high is attractive all through the year. The flowers, inconspicuous, are dotted about the plant in summer and the prickly fruits or burrs (burs) are crimson and bright in winter. Although the plant is chosen primarily for covering a flat rock, it may be grown in a pocket and used there as a groundwork or underplanting for early flowering bulbs such as *Crocus susianus* (orange flowers striped with dark purplish-brown), the crocuses springing up through the tight mat of bronze foliage: the result being a pleasing patch of colour in midwinter. Don't use bulbs with untidy foliage such as the Grape Hyacinth (*Muscari*). *Acaena microphylla* is the best known species, the most popular and talked about and the one recommended by rock-garden experts before all the others. It wants a sandy, lightish loam, a warm position and some shade. Gardeners who have grown it for many years, say it does better in semi-shady places than in full sun and will flourish in the shade of trees.

Other kinds offered by nurseries (I quote from current alpine catalogues) are: *A. buchananii* from South Island, New Zealand. A low mat of greyish leaves in which grow large greenish-yellow-spined burrs only partly visible.

A. inermis (perhaps a variety of *A. microphylla*) makes a dense mat of bronze-green leaves and spineless brown burrs.

A. sanguisorbae, a rampant spreading, light green mat-plant with round heads of purplish flowers. Ideal for the interstices of a paved walk in a rockery. (See Chapter 7.) Both from New Zealand.

'Blue Haze': of hybrid origin and forming low mounds, 6 inches high, of attractive blue-grey 'ferny' foliage, interlaced with red stems. *Acaena* are among the easier rock plants to grow. Propagation by seeds in spring, or by division after flowering. The plants cost about 20p each.

Acantholimon, natives of hot sunny mountainous places in Asia and Asia Minor, are true alpines. They aren't seen in many rockeries—personally I don't know anybody who grows the two offered by nurseries—and they are said to be difficult. They need first and foremost full sun and a warm spot where the soil is really gritty, light and sandy. Damp and cold and prolonged wet seem to be their worst enemies. They grow well and flourish in places like Sardinia and Greece, but even there, near their natural habitats, they sometimes die away after a few years of cultivation.

Acantholimon glumaceum (furnished with glumes—chaff-like bracts that enclose the flowers of grasses), the best of the genus and the one obtainable from most nurseries; the other species are rather difficult to get and appear to be even more intractable in cultivation. This plant makes tufts of spiky dark green leaves that are sharp-pointed; the flowers are bright rose ($\frac{1}{2}$ inch across) and are borne in clusters on 6-inch scapes (stems). A very pretty, prickly-looking plant. Its popular name is 'Prickly Thrift'. This alpine is found wild in hot rocky mountainous places in Armenia; it is said to have been first discovered on Mount Ararat.

The other rockery species of the ninety-odd species known, is *A. venustum* (lovely, graceful), with charming vivid rose flowers larger than those of the other plant. The tufts of leaves are silver-grey in colour, 6 inches high, and more open than in *A. glumaceum*. Both bloom in summer.

Acantholimon are slow-growing plants and quite difficult to propagate. Seeds germinate very slowly—in fact seed sowing is a frustrating business. Most gardeners attempt a sort of layering by pushing the partially severed stems firmly down into gritty, leafy soil they heap on to them in September. They are left till spring when usually new roots will have formed.

These plants won't live long in places where there are long spells of cold damp wet weather. They cost about 25p each.

Achillea suitable for rock gardens are listed as true Alpines. And *A. ageratifolia*, one of the most attractive, is recommended for the moraine. (See Chapter 4, page 124.)

(The popular name of *Achillea* seems to be 'Yarrow'; but correctly it is used only for *A. millefolium*, a 2-foot tall herbaceous plant. 'Milfoil' is another name; and 'Sneezewort' is sometimes used for *A. ptarmica*.)

A. tomentosa, an alpine species, is a yellow sunny plant with tiny flat flower-heads that in a mass make a bright patch of colour in July and August. The plant often remains in bloom till September; and it is about 9 inches tall. The leaves, green and finely divided, are tomentose (covered with fine woolly hair) and make a pleasing edging of foliage to a herbaceous border when the soil and situation are right. The soil must be gritty and sandy (add some sifted leafmould to it to keep it open and warm) and the situation must be open and in full sun. The rock Achilleas need warm gardens and don't succeed in the north. Those species, as this one, that come from hot Southern Europe and from Asia need dry places, though they must be watered when they are first planted—if you plant them in the spring. The best place for *A. tomentosa* is in a dry sunny pocket. I've seen it grown low down in a rockery—actually not in a pocket but against a rock-face— with a sheet of blue, bell Campanulas trailing down the rock-face as a background.

A. umbellata (umbellate—arranged in flat clusters) has white flowers and small ovalish, lobed leaves, silvery and woolly. The plant is 5 inches tall and like the preceding *Achillea* ideally suited to a pocket: the flowers grow bunched up close and give a richer effect. It is a native of rocky mountain slopes in Greece.

The hybrid *A. lewisii* × 'King Richard' has grey-green foliage and heads of cream-yellow flowers; it is about the same height as the other two. Propagate these Achilleas by division. During excessive wet cover the plants with panes of glass rigged up on strong wires to keep the woolly leaves reasonably dry, otherwise they will begin to rot. Price of plants is about 20p each.

Adonis amurensis is recommended for growing in a pot or a pan in the alpine house, probably because it blooms so early (February) and would be safer there. The bright yellow flowers, 2 inches across, anemone-like, are borne on short stems that grow longer with age and may ultimately reach a height of 12 inches or more. The flowers can be protected by a pane of glass during bad spells of weather. The foliage, which unfolds later, is finely divided, fern-like and a deep fresh green.

Where to plant it? It comes from the Amur River region of East Siberia (*amurensis*) and therefore is subject to severe cold, snow, frost and wet. It does well close against a rock facing north, the roots set in deep loamy garden soil, as close to the rock as possible. The plant may grow skew-whiff but it will have a better chance of flowering more freely and safely. This is the favourite *Adonis* and the only one that appears in most catalogues—priced at 35p a plant.

Two others I have seen in rockeries are *A. pyrenaica*, with bright golden-yellow flowers in June; and *A. vernalis* (golden-yellow and daisy-like) in April. They both come from the warm southern parts of Europe. *Adonis* are difficult plants to propagate, often dying off when attempts are made to divide them; and seed is extremely slow to germinate; none the less it may be sown as soon as the seed-pods swell and before they ripen and become dry.

Aethionema are natives of mountainous parts of the Mediterranean region and are classed as true alpines; the one called 'Warley Rose' is a special favourite. It is well known to most gardeners and is regarded as a variety of *A. coridifolium*, a native of Asia Minor. (The popular name is 'Persian Candytuft'. Which seems to be used for all the species we grow in our rockeries.) Our species, named after the Coris plant (a plant with the habit of a Thyme) has tiny, glaucous, rather fleshy leaves and round heads of rose-lilac flowers that bloom in mid-June. The variety 'Warley Rose' mentioned above has deeper rose-coloured flowers that stand out well against the blue-green foliage. Both plants are seen at their best on a sunny slope, running between the rocks, and need a well-drained sandy, limy soil.

Other species grown are *A. grandiflorum*, with comparatively large heads of deep rose flowers, and *A. pulchellum,* rather like *A. coridifolium* and often used to trail down a wall. (See chapter 3 where both species are described.)

These *Aethionema* often suffer during a severe winter, so it will be wise to increase one's stock by taking cuttings in late summer. Insert the shoots in sandy soil in a covered frame. These shoots form after the plants have been trimmed to remove the dead flower-heads.

Cost of plants is about 23p each.

Allium is a large family, with species found mostly in the temperate regions of the Northern hemisphere. It is the Onion family and contains the common vegetable *Allium cepa* and the garlic, *A. cativum*. Less frequently grown in our gardens are the herbaceous kinds and those suitable for the rockery, and the reason may well be that they smell strong when they are fingered or when the stems or leaves are broken or bruised. The most attractive for the herbaceous border and blooming in May is the species *A. Rosenbachianum*, a 2-foot tall plant with spherical heads of purple-rose flowers, good to look at and need not be smelled or cut and brought indoors.

They are all bulbs and are best planted deep in light loamy soil and left to grow undisturbed till you want to increase your stock. Which is easily done by planting offshoots that grow on the parent bulbs.

The loveliest for the rock-garden is *A. narcissiflorum* from the Alps of Europe and from the Caucasus, in which parts of the world it is often found in screes; it is recommended for the garden moraine (see Chapter 4). The species has been long known in Britain and in 1888 was awarded a First Class Certificate by the R.H.S. The scapes (flower-stems) vary from 4 to 12 inches in height; the leaves, shorter and very narrow, are a pleasing shade

43

of green; and the flowers, bright rose and bell-shaped ($\frac{1}{2}$ inch long) come in round clusters at the end of the stems—like all the *Allium* flowers. They are at first nodding, then grow erect and are at their best in July. This is well worth remembering, since there is a scarcity of flowers and colour in the rockery at this time of the year. The plant needs a prominent place in order to show off its beauty. And it is more suitable for a large rockery than a small one. Plant it on a sunny slope if you can with some vertical rocks in the background. But you might find it does better in the moraine.

Other kinds for the rockery are *A. cyaneum* (blue), about 6 inches tall, with blue flower-heads in summer; charming in a pocket. *A. karataviense*, from Turkestan, with very broad blue-green leaves and white (sometimes bluish) flowers carried in dense, globose heads; it blooms in May. *A. ostrowskianum*, also from the Alps of Turkestan, has rose-coloured flowers in round clusters and long, flattish grey-green leaves. (These last two plants are named after a mountain range and a patron of botany respectively.) The rock-garden *Allium* associate well with the blue-grey tufted ornamental grass, *Festuca ovina glauca*.

Allium will appeal specially to busy gardeners who want something easy to grow. They can be planted and left undisturbed for years. The bulbs cost about 20p each.

Alyssum are trailing plants much favoured for wall-gardens; they are described fully in Chapter 3, page 98. Suffice it to say now that *A. saxatile* (growing among rocks) has been called one of the three most popular rockery plants grown in our gardens, the other two being *Arabis* and *Aubrietia* and they are all found usually draping vertical rocks or are used as an edging in an ordinary flower-border. They bloom simultaneously in spring and are often the only alpines grown in a small rockery. *A. saxatile*, commonly known as 'Gold Dust', looks magnificent grown as *Aethionema Var.* 'Warley Rose' (page 42) is sometimes grown, that is on a gentle slope between low parallel rocks forming a sort of gulley or miniature ravine. The rocks keep the massed flowers compact and therefore upright. For my part, I think the mass of rich golden-yellow is enough—beautiful and striking on its own; however, I have seen *Cheiranthus* ('Siberian Wallflowers'), with their rich glowing orange flowers grown as companion plants, not in a rock-gully or ravine but along a pathway through a large rockery, the *Cheiranthus* being set among the *Alyssum* in autumn—the usual planting-out time—and springing up 12 inches or more high out of the mass of golden-yellow flowers: a startling display of brilliant orange-yellow in early summer, something that arrests one's attention and makes one stand and stare for a moment or two. *Alyssum* need a light, sandy, leafy soil, or any lightish garden soil. Other species are given in Chapter 3 and most of them can be raised from seed quite cheaply.

Anacyclus depressus (depressed, flattened) comes from the Atlas Mountains in North Africa and is recommended by rockery experts for growing on a sunny ledge: on the flat surface stone, the plant can spread out its feathery, fern-like foliage and its open daisy-shaped flowers; the petals are white and coloured purple on the back. This daisy-like alpine flourishes in ordinary loamy soil; and the rock ledge on which it is grown should preferably be at the top of the rockery and level with the natural surface of the ground; the plant is set in the soil behind and level with the flat rock or ledge, on which it is to spread out its flowers and stems. A flattish plant about 2 inches high, blooming in early summer. It is perfectly hardy and likes plenty of sun and in my opinion looks best growing on its own: if you *do* want something to go with it, plant clumps of the dwarf, blue-grey grass *Festuca ovina glauca* behind it. I have already recommended this grass as a companion plant for some of the *Allium*. *Anacyclus depressus* can be got from most alpine nurseries and costs 20p a plant.

Androsace is a genus of about a hundred species, some high alpines and difficult to grow except in an alpine house. Nurseries offer about a dozen different kinds, costing between 20p and 25p each. One of the loveliest from the Swiss Alps (found at an altitude of about 7,000 feet), is *A. alpina*, a mat-like plant of rosettes completely covered with tiny single rose-pink flowers in June; it is seldom a success in cultivation but several gardeners I know have grown it and got it to thrive in pans in their alpine houses. There are many species like this.

The species recommended for the average English garden is

A. sarmentosa (having runners, as in the Strawberry plant), a native of the Himalaya and of the mountains of Szechwan, South-West China. It is very beautiful with its round heads of tiny rose-coloured flowers borne on woolly stems 4 inches tall, these rising up from rosettes of silvery leaves; later with age the leaves become greener and smoother. The runners (stolons) spread out and are up to 5 inches long; they quickly root in sandy leafy soil and produce new plants. This species and its varieties belong to the Tufted Section (*Chamaejasme*) and are among the easiest of the *Androsace* to grow. They prosper in light sandy well-drained soil containing plenty of grit; some do best in the moraine. The variety 'Chumbyi' is one of these. As for the type—the species itself—it is said to grow anywhere (which is an exaggeration): it thrives and looks best on its own in a pocket of gritty leafy soil low down in the rock-garden where it can be easily seen and best enjoyed. It flowers in May and June and if any plant is wanted to go with it, the varieties seem to me to be the ideal choice: 'Galmont's Variety': large clear pink flowers and compact growth. 'Salmon's Variety': it much resembles the type but is a larger, more vigorous plant. *Var. yunnanensis* has small rosettes and smaller flowers than the other varieties. During prolonged spells of wet in winter, protect these hairy-leaved plants with panes of glass.

Other *Androsace* obtainable are: *A. carnea*, from the Alps, with tufts of greyish leaves and rose-coloured flowers marked with yellow; it blooms in May; the variety *brigantiaca*, a taller plant, with white tinted pink flowers; this is found on grassy slopes of the Mont Cenis Pass. They both flourish in deep, leafy, loamy soil that has plenty of grit in it (I have seen them growing well in this mixture and the surface covered with granite chips); *A. lanuginosa*, a silver-leaved trailer, with bunches of small pinkish-white flowers with a yellow eye, like tiny Verbena flowers, is best on a rock wall. See Chapter 3, page 98.

Propagation is by seed, cuttings, runners or by division of the tufts according to the type of plant.

The popular name 'Rock Jasmine' was given perhaps because the individual flowers resemble those of a miniature Jasmine—five-petalled and star-like.

Anemone are special favourites with people who possess a wild garden, for many species like cool shady places, cool damp soil, and plenty of room in which to increase and spread. The smallest kinds, not more than 6 inches tall, are the best for the rock-garden, though they spread rapidly and too far for a limited space. (Under the genera *Hepatica* and *Pulsatilla* will be found other Anemone-like plants; they were formerly classed with *Anemone*.)

The Wood Anemone, found wild in Britain, can get into one's garden through its roots being present in the leafmould one collects from under trees: that's how mine arrived. With its small white flowers, this Anemone is very well known. It is not particularly striking. A rapid spreader and almost as rampant as the Welsh Poppy (*Meconopsis cambrica*). I have seen it growing in an alpine lawn, thick round the shady side of a large rockery. It blooms in March and then later in early summer disappears altogether, but springs up stronger than ever the following year. There are pink and also blue varieties that are more sought after than the common white. Its specific name is *Anemone nemorosa* (inhabiting shady places).

A. blanda (pleasing) is a native of Europe and the Taurus in Asia. It has deep blue flowers (2 inches across) in winter or early spring. On that account it is prized by gardeners and often grown close against a rock-face that provides the necessary warmth and protection it needs. The plant is often less than 6 inches tall and spreads as rapidly as *A. nemorosa*. Like that plant however it conveniently disappears in early summer and other things spring up and take its place. Both these Anemones, although grown in rock-gardens, are essentially woodland plants. Two species widely recommended for the rockery are *A.A. narcissiflora* and *sylvestris*. The first, from all parts of the world, is a variable plant, from 6 to 20 inches tall, with clusters of flowers that are sometimes white or cream or purplish and usually stand erect on their stems against deeply-toothed green leaves. They bloom in May. The variety *monantha* is single-flowered and there are hairy forms from the high mountains of Asia. Hillier offers the type: 'Flowers in umbels (clusters), white with yellow anthers; May to July; price 20p a plant.'

47

A. sylvestris or *A. silvestris* (of a wood or forest) has satiny white, slightly drooping flowers, 1½ inches across when fully open; they are fragrant and come on longish stems rising from dark green leaves. A lovely, graceful plant for a moist, shady corner in the rock-garden, where the soil is deep, light and leafy. It blooms in April and spreads as many of the Anemones do. I have seen a clump in bloom against a vertical boulder of Heatherstone Rock facing due north, the pink-grey colour of the rock providing a delightful background to the white flowers.

Like the other spreading kinds of Anemones, this species is easily propagated by planting out pieces of the rootstock in September or about that time. But most of these rampant plants will look after themselves, increasing rapidly on their own. *A. narcissiflora* is best propagated by seed.

The popular name of *A. sylvestris* is the 'Snowdrop Windflower'. 'Windflower' is used for all Anemones apparently; the name has nothing to do with cultural requirements or habitats: simply the generic name is derived from the Greek word *anemone* daughter of the wind.

Antennaria dioica (dioecious: having the male and female flowers on separate plants) is a mat-forming alpine—a rock-coverer or creeper—from the high mountains of Europe, Asia and North America. (The popular name is 'Cat's Ear'). There are several species and varieties, the best known being *A. dioica* 'Rosea', with grey woolly leaves (1 inch long) on creeping growths, and clusters of pink flowers coming in June on stems 2 to usually 4 inches high. An attractive plant to cover a flat rock or a piece of light, sandy soil where other things are planted. They will grow up through the mat of foliage before the flowers come or after they've gone. (Winter-flowering bulbs such as Snowdrops or Crocuses would come long before the *Antennaria* blooms and perhaps some of the late Cyclamen could follow in autumn; no doubt the reader will be able to think of something equally lovely as companion plants.) I have seen this *Antennaria* most often used for decorating crazy-paving walks or for more formal stone pathways. (See Chapter 7, page 162.)

Anthemis montana (of the mountains), one of the so-called 'Chamomiles', comes from the hot regions of the Mediterranean and from Syria on the borders of Jordan and Iraq. It is the species specially recommended for the rockery, a cushion-forming plant with white daisy-like flower-heads and hairy, divided leaves. The form Var. *aetnensis* is a prettier plant and prized for its pink flowers. Both bloom in late summer and need a light leafy soil and a warm sunny position. Both may be grown together as companion plants.

A. cupaniana, from Italy and Southern Europe, makes a large spreading mass of aromatic silver-grey foliage studded with daisy-like flowers 2 inches across, like wild Marguerites. It is in bloom right from June till December, and therefore a valuable rock-plant to have; but its 3-foot wide cushions are unfortunately too large for the average rockery. It is related to *A. montana* but taller and bigger than that plant.

The genuine 'Chamomile' is *A. nobilis*, found wild in Britain, and the species recommended for making a lawn (see Chapter 8, pages 171–2); and its flowers are infused in boiling water to make the well-known Chamomile Tea.

These 'Chamomile' are increased by division or by cuttings. The plants cost about 20p each.

A. carpatica, from the high Alps of Southern Europe, resembles *A. montana*, but has larger flowers, solitary (one to each stem) and leaves that are irregularly divided into larger segments than the other species. So far I have found it difficult to get.

Anthyllus are sun-loving plants from the Alps of Central and Southern Europe. *Anthyllus montana*, perhaps the best known, is found on limestone rocks and in cultivation revels in sunny places and sandy soils containing lime. It is a mat-forming deciduous plant, not more than 4 inches high, with silvery hairy foliage, and rosy-pink flowers in clover-like heads on shortish stems. There are several varieties, the one usually offered by nurseries being *A. montana var. rubra*, with deep rose clover-like flowers which are at their best in May and June.

A. hermanniae is a deciduous shrublet, usually not much more than 2 feet tall, with yellow and orange-red pea-flowers; it needs a warm sunny niche or recess in a part of a rock-garden that faces due south where it will get plenty of protection during a severe winter; for this *Anthyllus*, like some of the other shrubby

49

kinds, is on the tender side in inland districts. It is a native of
Corsica and rather expensive: a plant costs about 75p. *A. montana*
about 30p. Both should be propagated by cuttings taken in
August. They root more easily under glass.

Antirrhinum glutinosum is a trailer, only half-hardy, and described
in Chapter 3, pages 99, along with other wall plants. It did not
prove a success in the rockery built and planted by Camillo Luca
at Beaconsfield, Bucks., mentioned in the previous chapter, page
17. But what did well were the 'Tom Thumb' varieties of 'Snapdragon', seeds of which were sown in crevices.

Aphyllanthes monpeliensis, is another rock-plant which needs
special care; it is best housed in the alpine house. (See Chapter 5,
page 136.)

Aquilegia: The name is well known to all gardeners who have
flower-borders. And the herbaceous kinds are almost invariably
called 'Columbines'. These are varieties of *Aquilegia vulgaris*, many
hybrids and strains of which are now on the market; and they
are perhaps quite suitable for large rockeries, planted close against
vertical rocks that show up their colours admirably. The so-called
'Hensol Harebell' is said to be a hybrid of *A. alpina* and *A.
vulgaris* and has deep blue flowers on stems 18 inches to 2 feet tall.
A clump of these enchanting blue 'Columbines' looks magnificent
against grey-white limestone rocks.

Most alpine nurseries offer about half a dozen different species;
and *A. alpina* usually comes first on their lists. In my opinion it
is the loveliest, and in the wild it is strong and rampant but in
cultivation one of the most intractable of the race. *A. alpina*
(alpine; above the timber-line) is found on the Swiss Alps and
abundant on the montane herbage of the Mont Cenis Pass at an
altitude of about 6,800 feet. The flowers are short-spurred and at
their best in May. They are often 3 inches wide and come on
stems 12 inches tall. The leaves are a dark green and deeply
divided.

A. flabellata (like an open fan: alluding to the shape of the
leaves) is a native of Japan and considered by many rock-garden
enthusiasts to be as lovely as *A. alpina*. And it is, I think, when
it is seen massed in a pocket against a bare rock. The flowers are
white tinged with lavender and carried on shortish stems that

rise out of thick, basal glaucous leaves. These *Aquilegia* need a leafy sandy moist loam and are best raised from seeds collected from the plants themselves or obtained from alpine specialists who import the seed from the countries where the plants grow wild. Both *Aquilegia alpina* and *A. flabellata* last longer in bloom when they are grown in partial shade. They cost about 25p each.

Arabis and *Arenaria* are mostly represented in our gardens by *Arabis albida flore-pleno*, the Double White Arabis or 'Rock Cress'; and *Arenaria balearica* or the 'Sandwort', and being trailers or creepers are well adapted to wall gardens and more often seen and grown there than in the ordinary rockery (see Chapter 3, pages 99–100, where both plants are described). My favourite *Arabis* is *A. blepharophylla*, with rough leaves and very attractive rose-purple flowers; but it is too tender for most gardens and best grown in the alpine house (Chapter 5).

Armeria are the 'Thrifts', among the most popular of all our alpine plants. The best is the exiguous *Armeria caespitosa* and its varieties or cultivars (raised in the nurseries) and of course like all the choicest plants, or nearly all of them, difficult to grow outside; this exquisite race* is most successful when planted in pans in the alpine house or given scree conditions in the rockery. But our native species *A. maritima* is a charming little tufted plant sometimes used for edging in an ordinary herbaceous border; in the rockery I plant it with the blue-grey ornamental grass *Festuca ovina glauca*: they go well together. And in winter the variety *A. maritima variegata*, with golden-yellow spiky leaves gives an extra bit of colour when all the flowers are dead; 'Alba' has small heads of white flowers; and 'Vindictive' deep pink; they bloom through June and July. The specific epithet gives a clue to this species' habitat and we find many of these little plants along our coasts: 'Sea Pinks' we call them. *Armeria* like a sandy, loamy soil and sunny places. The 'Mountain Thrift', *A. montana* from the European Alps, a smaller plant with pinkish-lilac flower-heads, is lovely massed on its own in a pocket. To propagate these plants: divide them in late summer and let the pieces root under glass.

* 'Alba' (white); 'Beechwood' (deep pink); 'Bevan's Variety' (deep rose) are three of the best.

51

Arnica montana is the 'Mountain Tobacco', a true alpine from the mountains of Southern Europe and, like *Aquilegia alpina*, doesn't give of its best in cultivation. Nevertheless I've known rock-gardening enthusiasts grow it very successfully in a pocket of deep peaty gritty soil in full sun. 'We grow it,' says an alpine nursery, 'for its remarkable orange-yellow daisy-like flowers which often measure more than 2 inches across . . .' The flower-stems about 8 inches tall spring up from a tuft or rosette of flattish oblong leaves; these tufts may be divided in spring to provide new plants. But once this mountain orange daisy-like plant has settled down, it is best left undisturbed. It costs about 25p from alpine specialists, who can usually provide seed.

Artemisia may be called foil plants, that is plants that play the part of companions or background plants to those that flower—the *Festuca* mentioned in previous pages is a favourite foil plant. But many rock-gardeners rightly regard these silver-white finely-divided fern-like *Artemisias* as beautiful enough to stand on their own against a rock and indeed as beautiful and far more permanent than many things that flower. There are several species to choose from: *Artemisia mutellina* is found at high altitudes in the mountains of central and southern Europe and varies from 2 to 8 inches in height; it has finely-divided soft, silver-white leaves coming on inch-long stalks and in August small heads of pale yellow flowers that are usually cut off by gardeners who prefer to see only the lacy silvery foliage. It is not obtainable at all nurseries, but *A. lanata* (woolly) is; they may offer it as *A. pedemontana*; it comes from the same regions as the other plants and is of tufted habit, about 2 inches high, but has longish—4- to 8-inch—flowering spikes; the fern-like foliage is silver-white and lovely in a mass, say, growing in a pocket above another full of blue Gentians. A cool patch of colour for the rockery. *Artemisia* like a leafy loamy soil and the tufty kinds may be divided, or cuttings may be taken to increase the stock of plants. The foliage of most *Artemisia* is aromatic and the larger kinds are often used for cutting. *A. stelleriana,* familiarly known in Cornwall (where it is naturalized) as 'Beach Wormwood', is grown by some people on a rock-wall and looks very effective there with its trailing whitish foliage. The plants cost about 25p each.

Arthropodium candidum is a rarity in our rockeries; it is a plant with grass-like leaves (12 inches tall) and 4-inch spikes of pretty white flowers; it is decidedly tender around London; it makes a charming pot plant however and is mostly grown in the alpine house. (See Chapter 5.)

Asarina procumbens still appears in catalogues but the correct name is *Antirrhinum asarina* and the plant is grown either on a wall as a 'strong trailer' or in the alpine house because it is rather tender or, at least, likes more sun and warmth than it normally gets in an English garden.

Asarum are mostly grown in the wild-garden where they can be used as ground-covering plants; they have attractive leaves but uninteresting flowers. Two species are obtainable and are excellent for a miniature water-garden that is part of a large rockery (Chapter 8).

Asperula suberosa is an alpine plant that all my rock-gardening friends long to grow successfully outside but so far have failed. With its silvery, woolly leaves and tiny tubular pink flowers, it has a curiously-artificial look and is an enchanting plant. The alpine house or the moraine is the most suitable place for it and for the other few members of the family obtainable.

Asters that grow in our borders are varieties planted for the late show of flowers: we can pick them often in November. In the rockery there are several from the high mountains of the world and the species usually grown and found most amenable to English rock-garden conditions is *Aster alpinus* from the European Alps. About 6 inches tall and of spreading habit, it has bright purple flowers (1 to 2 inches wide) and ovalish green radical leaves (growing from the crown of the plant, like a rosette) and a few small leaves on the stems. Many charming varieties have been produced. 'Roseus', with rose-mauve flowers is lovely through the early summer. The plants like a light, leafy, sandy soil, I find; propagation is by division in late summer, as soon as the flowers have faded.

Astilbe are feathery-looking plants popularly but erroneously called Spiraeas; two of them, like the *Asarum*, make charming little plants for the rockery water-garden. They are described in chapter 8.

Aubrietia has been called Britain's favourite rockery plant.
Perhaps it is. At least it is found in practically every garden
in the British Isles, I imagine; and not always of course in a
rockery; one sees it edging flower-borders, smothering lovelier
things near it . . . It is a natural trailer and therefore best on a
wall.

B

Bellis is the Daisy family and contains some charming miniature
kinds, viz. *Bellis perennis* 'Dresden China' and 'Rob Roy' (pink
and double crimson flowers respectively); but none, strange
enough, is recommended for the rockery. It has been suggested
that they are too formal-looking (ideal for bedding-out) and too
set and 'prim' to grow among alpine plants. There is a gem
called the 'Blue Daisy'; it comes from the mountain heights of
Morocco and has bluish flowers on 3-inch stems that rise up from
ovalish leaves and blooms in summer. Unfortunately it is rather
tender; it needs a warm, semi-shady crevice and flourishes more
luxuriantly in the south of France than in the south of England.
It can be brought successfully through a bad winter however by
covering it with a bell glass. Its name is *Bellis rotundifolia caerulescens* (roundish-shaped leaves; bluish flowers) but the plant is not
listed in any current alpine catalogue I have consulted. It was
introduced from the Atlas Mountains (North Africa) in 1872.
People who grow it prefer to keep it in an alpine house. Sandy
soil is best.

Bolax, botanists say, should really be *Azorella*. And the few
species are apparently now described under that name. Nurseries
list *B. glebaria*, however, and Hillier describes it: 'A tufted cushion-
like plant thriving in a sunny position; flowers greenish-yellow
not very conspicuous; spring—3 ins. 20p.' Farrer doesn't mention it (*The English Rock-Garden*) or any of the race. The R.H.S.
Dictionary gives only this plant—with the cushion habit of an
Androsace. It needs light, gritty soil and a warm open position.
Is often grown in paved walks and on steps.

C

Going through the list of C-plants, we single out at once the Campanulas as the best known and probably the favourite family. *Calamintha* ('Calamint'); *Calandrinia* ('Rock Purslane'); *Calceolaria* ('Slipper Flower') and *Cyclamen* I've seen in a good number of rock-gardens; but none of the tiny Chrysanthemums or the *Convolvulus, Crassula,* or the trailing *Cyananthis.* And there are others as little known as these. Farrer describes a good many that are never grown in the average rock-garden. Crocuses, which appear only in Bulb Catalogues, he includes of course; but they make the best show planted in drifts or sweeps in short grass; wild-gardens; alpine lawns.

First the 'Calamints'; *Calamintha alpina*, with small violet-coloured flowers in whorls, grows 6 inches high, and is recommended for a dry wall. *C. grandiflora* has 2-inch coarsely-toothed leaves, purplish-rose flowers in loose racemes on stems 18 inches tall, and blooms in summer: earlier than the other. Ordinary sandy soils and a sunny place are needed. Both plants are very easily propagated by division of the roots.

Calandrinia umbellata (in umbels). The flowers—$\frac{3}{4}$ inch across—come in terminal clusters or umbels and are a hard magenta-crimson, a colour which many people don't like. The plant, 6 inches high, is recommended for warm, sunny, sandy places in rockeries and for wall-gardens; the flowers close up in dull weather. A native of Peru and not always amenable to cultivation in our country, it is often raised annually from seed. You can get a good specimen for 20p and the *Calamintha* cost about the same.

Some of the rockery 'Slipper Flowers' are classed as true alpines; they come from high mountainous regions of South America. And as they need deep, cool, moist soils, are best grown in or near the water-garden, which may be part of a rock-garden; or they may be grown where running water flows through the garden: against a rock, say, sunk in peaty, well-drained soil. *Calceolaria polyrrhiza* (having many roots) has small yellow slipper flowers (an inch long) with purplish spots. It is a creeping plant, making a spreading mat of leaves, from which arise the 6-inch stems carrying usually one or two flowers. The plant likes partial shade and is usually increased by root division.

If one were asked to name the next favourite alpine after *Arabis, Aubrietia* and *Alyssum*, I think it would be *Campanula portenschlagiana*. It is one of those rock-plants that do well and look well in practically any part of the garden. It can be used in the border along with the tall border types (*C. persicifolia* and the Canterbury Bells: *C. medium*). Plant it in clumps in front of them. It can also be grown in the greenhouse or the conservatory along with the more tender 'Chimney Bell-flower': *C. pyramidalis*, which in warm moist atmospheres will grow nearly as tall as you. Plant it in a tub as a groundwork and let the tall flowers come up through it; the white *C. pyramidalis alba* looks very attractive with it.

Our plant (named in honour of the Austrian botanist Fr. Elder von Portenschlag-Ledermeyer) has light blue-purple bells on 6-inch stems and smooth light green leaves. For a companion plant try the yellow-flowered (tiny flowers) creeping Nasturtium, *Tropaeolum polyphyllum*, with grey-green stems and foliage. It needs a really warm sheltered place and is less hardy than the Campanula *and* far more expensive—90p a plant: the Campanula, like most of the other alpine kinds, costs about 20p. All the bellflowers do well in sandy loamy soils and prosper in partial shade—better for them than full sun. First-year plants are best well watered regularly during dry weather. It is an accommodating plant, grows and looks well at the foot of a boulder; or in a pocket (the rocks surrounding a mass of flowers pressed close together); or set in the crevices of a wall-garden where the plants have the appearance of a single trailer, the bells covering the face of the wall—this is where it should be grown along with the creeping yellow Nasturtium. There are at least another dozen well-known alpine species. From my experience I find that *C. cochlearifolia* (spoon-shaped leaves) is one of the most popular. I see it in many gardens in this district—South Bucks. It is still known to many people and nurseries as *C. pusilla*. The bells are very small, blue or white in colour and the stems short, about 4 inches; the leaves small, ovalish and toothed. It is a beautiful bellflower but an obstinate spreader and in time may prove something of a problem, especially where there are other plants growing near. You can pull it up; I've done it and found it doesn't suffer much: it grows just as strongly again. The tiny nodding blue or white bells look especially attractive on a low rock-wall.

Nurseries list another twenty-odd species, all suitable for the rock-garden.

Some unfortunately are eaten immediately by slugs and disappear the first year; they should be grown in trough- or sink-gardens (Chapter 6): *Campanula zoysii*,* with tiny tubular blue bells, is one of these and seems to be attacked more quickly than any other rock-plant; it needs, by the way, a rich loamy soil containing plenty of grit or chips and some lime. All the *Campanulas* flourish in limy soils. One last word about them: you can grow the tall 'Chimney Bellflower' in the crevices of a wall-garden—surprisingly enough! The important thing to remember is that the wall must be fairly tall and slope backwards.

Cerastium tomentosum (tomentose: woolly) is 'Snow-in-Summer', the well-known grey-silvery-leaved plant with ordinary-looking white flowers on 6-inch stems, these and the leaves being covered with whitish hairs. Like *Campanula cochlearifolia*, it spreads by underground stems, but is much stronger than that plant and soon becomes a nuisance in rockeries and on walls. It needs a dry sunny bank to itself; poor, starved soil produces whiter growths and foliage.

Ceratostigma plumbaginoides (resembling a Plumbago) is a dwarf, shrubby rockery plant, the hardiest of several species, and is grown specially for its blue flowers, which bloom in September. It comes from China—was found on the walls in Pekin—but is not often seen in our gardens. It is cheap enough (20p) and succeeds in sandy loams in warm, sunny places. It may need winter protection in some districts. The stems are red and the foliage assumes this colour in autumn. Propagation is by root-division. The plant sometimes appears in catalogues as *Plumbago larpentae*.

Chrysanthemums for the rock-garden are even rarer. *C. argenteum* (silvery) and *C. densum* are the only two listed in most catalogues.

* This species is rather difficult to get nowadays. See also chapter 5, page 137.

(The alpine Asters, with similar flowers, are better known, page
53.) *Chrysanthemum argenteum* (silvery) is a greyish-white-looking
plant, 6 inches tall, with aromatic leaves and white flowers that
are borne on single stems. Only striking, really, in a mass, in a
pocket in the rockery. It is common in the mountainous regions
of China and Japan. And *C. densum* (close, crowded) has tiny
single yellow flowers in clusters on stems 8 inches high; and
finely divided velvety hairy leaves. *C. densum amanum* (from the
Akmadagh-Amani Mountains, Northern Syria) is the variety
offered by most nurseries. The leaves are bright silver-white.
Both these *Chrysanthemums* are shrubby plants; both need deep
gritty perfectly-drained soils and a sunny position. Their daisy-
like flowers are very welcome in late summer and autumn. The
plants are easily propagated by division.

Cistus are 'Rock Roses' or 'Gum Cistus'—the stems and growths
of many kinds are sticky. All the plants are on the tender side and
flourish most luxuriantly in hot southern districts. Not many are
suitable for gardens around London. And as they make rather
big bushy shrubs, need plenty of room. The loveliest by far is
the hybrid *Cistus × purpureus* (a cross between *C. ladaniferus* and
C. villosus), with large single-rose-like flowers (3 inches across),
red-purple with a darker-coloured blotch at the base of each petal,
and a centre of golden-yellow stamens. A midsummer flowerer
like all the others. The individual blooms open at midday and
about eight hours later drop; but the blooms continue to come
day after day for many weeks. The stems and leaves, very narrow
and sage-green, are sticky and people always remark upon it when
they cut the branches—perhaps when pruning. The flowers, so
evanescent, are of course useless for indoor decoration. Pruning
and shaping are often necessary when the shrubs are grown in
limited spaces. *C. × purpureus* makes a rather untidy bush about
4 feet tall and as much across. The ideal place for it—and it
should be massed—is on a hot sunny slope in a big rock-garden
facing due south. The soil must be light, sandy and rather starved.
A sharp frost will kill the shrub at once. So always take cuttings
in late summer: small unflowered pieces are rooted in pots of
sandy soil in a greenhouse. On a high wall-garden it could be
planted at the top and allowed to grow over and down the front.

Which the shrub does very readily. Plant a clump of deep purple summer Irises (your choice) at the foot of the wall to go with the red-purple of the *Cistus*. A good specimen in a pot costs 50p.

Convolvulus are best on a wall where they can trail and show off their flowers to best advantage (Chapter 3). *Crassula* are on the tender side and the rock kinds are mostly grown in pots in the alpine house; but *C. sarcocaulis* (fleshy stemmed) is a valuable plant for rockeries, since it blooms in late summer and early autumn. According to the R.H.S. Dictionary: 'The only *Crassula* that can be grown out of doors without protection in this country.' It is a smallish shrubby plant with small pointed green leaves and pink flowers in branched clusters. A warm sunny place, such as it gets in its native South Africa, is necessary, and well-drained gritty soil. Propagation is by seeds, or by cuttings, using 3-inch stems. Root them (and sow seeds) indoors. Crocuses are best in the wild-garden, water-garden and alpine lawn. The winter species are valuable for the show they give in January, February and March, before much else is moving. *Cyclamen*, like *Crocuses*, are best naturalized and the open woodland is the ideal place for them. They all like partial shade and flourish luxuriantly in slightly limy soil with pebbly rubble in it. *C. neapolitanum* is regarded as the most valuable species for the average garden since it blooms in autumn and often till winter, and sends up its flowers (small, rose blotched with carmine) before the leaves that are usually very pretty with silver marbling on shades of green— some light, some dark. In parts of the country you will find this little *Cyclamen* naturalized in mossy leafy ground. In the rockery it should be grown in a semi-shady place, say, in a spot facing north-west with a large boulder in the background.

Although the corms are obtainable from most nurseries specializing in alpines (corms cost about 20p each; the white-flowered variety *album* 60p!) you can get good seed at 10p a packet; and seed is often the best way to establish a colony of these lovely plants. (Dobies' offer 'Mixed Rose-pink or white flowers with beautiful silver-marbled foliage. Hardy perennial; 6–9 inches; July–November; 8p a packet.') The corms must be set about 2 inches under the soil. Never disturb these hardy *Cyclamen* once they are thriving. They grow wild in Southern Europe—France, Italy, Greece.

A lovely association consists of rose-carmine *Cyclamen* growing in front of clumps of deep blue Gentians: *Gentiana sino-ornata* blooms in late autumn and is now very well known. It won't tolerate lime, so plant it in a compost of sifted leafmould and silver sand—well behind the *Cyclamen*.

For winter and early spring there is *C. coum*, with very dark green roundish leaves in late autumn and carmine flowers in January. A choice little flower—4 inches high—for a sheltered nook.

D

'D' plants seem to be rather uncommon—apart from *Dianthus* (Alpine Pinks) one species of which I suppose everybody grows; this is our native 'Cheddar Pink', *Dianthus gratiano-politanus* (of the neighbourhood of Grenoble)—it is fairly common in many parts of Central Europe.

Daphnes are too difficult for most people. *D. petraea*, from the high mountains of Southern Europe, is greatly admired and desired by all who see it in bloom but very few can grow it. The R.H.S. says 'Both it and its variety (*grandiflora*) are usually grown in an alpine-house.'

Delphinium grandiflorum and its varieties are easy; they are strongly recommended for the rockery, where they provide in late summer striking patches of pure vivid blue, rivalled only by a carpet of blue Gentians, which are never easy to grow. These dwarf Delphiniums are about a foot high, branching plants covered with rich blue flowers almost hiding the narrow green leaves. The plants need deep lightish loamy soil and plenty of sun and always protection from slugs. They can be raised from seed (7p a packet) and many gardeners treat them as annuals and raise new stocks every year. Sow in January, under glass, for plants to bloom the same year. A big clump looks magnificent low down in the rockery. Think of some yellow-flowered alpine to go with it.

Dianthus alpinus (the Alpine Pink of the Austrian Alps) is called by many collectors and by those who have seen it growing in its natural habitat 'The most precious of the race . . .' The plant, about 4 inches high, forms a spreading grass-green mat covered in summer (June to August usually) with flesh-coloured or deep pink flowers an inch or so across. The only slight disappointment is that the flowers aren't scented—one imagines all Pinks smell. Hillier's catalogue describes it as having 'Large red flowers hiding the tufted green leaves; May–June; 3 inches; 25p'. In most rockeries it is not easy to establish; it needs a moist, light, leafy soil with a generous admixture of lime rubble. And above all the drainage must be perfect. Some gardeners prefer to grow it in the moraine. I've seen it flourishing in a pocket in a rock-garden near London, where it got some shade during midday; and also in the crevice of a low wall-garden.

Our native 'Cheddar Pink' is no trouble at all and will grow and thrive practically anywhere: in the rockery (pocket or crevice); in a wall crevice; at the top of a wall; and of course as an edging plant in a flower-border. Light, sandy, limy soil is best and it is easy to propagate. You can divide Pinks up or raise them from seed. Other easy kinds are *D. deltoides*,* the 'Maiden Pink' (6 inches tall), with purplish-crimson flowers; *D. neglectus* (6 inches), with rose-red toothed petals with a buff reverse, and small narrow, stiff leaves that form a close mat; it blooms in late summer; (*neglectus* in English is 'disregarded', meaning the plant was hitherto overlooked).† It dislikes lime. *D. squarrosus* (botanical term referring to the type of leaf), a tufted Pink from South Russia, with pale rose feathery petals; a fragrant plant. And there are dozens of very beautiful hybrids of these species: all good rockery Pinks and all easy to grow. Well rooted specimens can be got for about 25p each. Owners of low wall-gardens might like to cover it—almost—with these charming Pinks; many are seen to best advantage on, or trailing down, a wall face.

Draba aizoides (Aizoon-like evergreen) is attractive not only

---

* The word means shaped like the Greek letter $\triangle$. More or less triangular in shape. The leaves are narrowed to a wedge-shaped base.

† Another explanation is that the plant is inconspicuous when the flowers are closed.

for its tiny bright yellow flowers, but for its rosettes of moss-like foliage. In April the plant sends up 3-inch stems with yellow flowers and it looks well and thrives on Tufa rock. It is a native of Central Europe and is found wild in some parts of Britain. A light, open, leafy soil is necessary and a sunny place; and propagation is by seeds or by removing rosettes in late summer. The popular name is 'Whitlow Grass'.

Dryas octopetala (having eight petals) is another native plant, though, like the other: rare. It is known to collectors as the 'Mountain Avens'. The flowers ($1\frac{1}{2}$ inches across) rather resemble small white Anemones with yellow stamens or miniature Dog Roses and come thickly in May and June, almost hiding the foliage; the leaves are oblongish, 1 inch long, and deep green above and white and hairy beneath; in late summer the seeds form, silvery-white and feathery and are singularly attractive against the bare rocks. Ordinary lightish soil suits it and it should be top-dressed with sifted leafmould in late winter. The stems root easily by layering themselves in the soil. It is also raised by cuttings and by seeds. Once established, the plant must not be disturbed. Let it spread mat-like and fill a good-sized pocket.

E

*Edraianthus** are Campanula-like plants from the regions of the Mediterranean and the Balkans and have been described as more beautiful than the genuine bellflowers. They require a warm sunny place and very deep soil to grow in, since they have long foraging roots that go down to a good depth. Give the plants a mixture of equal parts of loam, sifted leafmould and limestone chips. Propagation is usually by cuttings which are taken in summer and rooted under glass.

E. serpyllifolius (with Thyme-like leaves) comes from the southern parts of the Balkan Peninsula. The variety offered is usually 'Major', a gem with purple-blue bell-shaped flowers nearly 1 inch long on 6-inch stems; the leaves come in rosettes

* See Chapter 4, 'The Moraine', page 125.

and form in time an attractive spreading mat. The important thing is to keep plenty of chips in the soil and round the plant as it grows and develops and not to put it in the ordinary soil that would suit the better known Campanulas. I have seen several species of *Edraianthus* growing well both in an alpine house and in the scree; many gardeners prefer to grow them this way. By the way, you will sometimes find *Edraianthus* described under *Wahlenbergia*, to which family they are very closely related. (See page 92.)

Erigeron have the popular name of 'Fleabane' and were said to have been used in the past 'for smoking off fleas'. *E. mucronatus* is the one prized by most rock-gardeners and is nearly always grown on a wall.

E. aurantiacus (orange): its popular name is 'Orange Daisy': and the plant is perhaps more often seen in the flower-border than in the rockery but it is useful there among the grey rocks. About 12 inches tall with velvety foliage and daisy-like orange flowers 2 inches across, blooming in summer; it should be planted in a pocket low down in a sunny spot. *E. leiomerus* (smooth) has small leaves, smooth and shining, forming tufts, from which arise on 4-inch stems the flowers ($\frac{3}{4}$ inch across) of an exquisite shade of lavender-blue that has a curiously beautiful sheen. A charming little Daisy-plant for a warm sunny pocket with well drained soil that doesn't dry out. The species comes from the Rocky Mountains. Hillier describes it: 'Tiny lavender-blue daisies. Easy and beautiful; June; 4 inches.' Propagation is by seeds or by root division.

Eriogonum umbellatus, like the 'Orange Daisy', is a good choice for the rockery because it blooms late, when most other things have finished—and it is not at all common. The flowers, yellow and small, come in umbels on stems about 6 inches high and are usually at their best in September. The plant forms a spreading evergreen carpet (the leaves green above and downy beneath) and provides a delightful setting for some of the winter flowering alpine Crocuses. The species is a native of British Columbia.

Euphorbia myrsinites (resembling Myrtle) is often recommended for walls but is really more satisfactory and looks lovelier planted in a pocket high up in a rockery, where it can trail over the sides.

The stems are prostrate, about 12 inches long, bending over with the weight of the fleshy, blue-grey leaves (perhaps almost the colour of Myrtle leaves) and the 3-inch clusters of flowers with conspicuous yellow-green bracts. A beautiful plant at its best in June and July. Rather tender, however, in cold gardens; it is worth raising extra plants from seed annually. Seeds germinate easily under glass. The popular name of the Euphorbias is 'Spurge' or 'Milkworts'—our species is a native of Southern Europe and is particularly common in the mountains of Corsica.

G

Gazania ('Treasure Flower') are half-hardy perennials recommended by some gardeners for the rockery. My nursery says: 'South African plants with very large brightly coloured Daisies. Require winter protection in all but the mildest areas. Excellent plants for seaside and hot, sunny situations. 4 inches. R.' ('R' indicating that the plant is especially suitable for rock-gardens.) You can buy a good specimen of *G.* × *splendens* (gleaming) in a pot for 25p and it can be planted out any time during the summer. This hybrid has stems spreading from the base, narrowish leaves, green above, silky-white beneath, and striking daisy-blooms, 3 inches or more across, orange with a black centre. Full sun for this late summer flowerer. And as one can't rely on it to survive our winters, one must raise new stock from seed annually (cost: about 10p a packet). The soil should consist of equal parts of loam and powdered peat or leafmould. *Gazania* are also mentioned on page 24.

Gentians call up memories of the Swiss Alps and the myriads of flowers growing there. Every few steps upward and one comes across a patch of glowing blue in the grass, which is usually *Gentiana verna*. And this is the species everybody wants to grow in their gardens. And it is the most difficult and often dismissed by gardeners as an impossible plant. Yet nearly every nurseryman specializing in alpines offers it—it can be got for 25p in a pot—and it is described simply as 'One of the glories of the Alps. Vivid blue, star-shaped flowers.' Most people leave it in its pot

Chiastophyllum oppositifolium, a charming rock garden plant, with tiny yellow flowers. Good for walls.

Vinca minor (page 173), one of the blue dwarf varieties useful for growing in an Alpine Lawn.

Star of Bethlehem (*Ornithogalum umbellatum*), white star flowers for the wilder part of the rock garden.

Lewisia howellii, a so-called "difficult alpine" and usually chosen for a warm, protected crevice or for the Alpine House.

Sempervivum tectorum var. triste, a Houseleek for a dry crevice; and lovely enough for a pot indoors.

Gentiana sino-ornata, the beautiful autumn Gentian, with deep blue trumpet-flowers. Must have a lime-free soil. See page 65.

and put it in an alpine house. The finest specimens I've seen in cultivation have been grown there. And the owners have always sown seed as soon as it is ripe so as to have a stock of new plants on hand. It seems short-lived however one treats it . . .

The best known is the one that for years was called *G. acaulis*, but is now *G. excisa* in catalogues. With the exception of the Chinese *G. sino-ornata*, it is the Gentian seen in the vast majority of rock-gardens. But although it makes a healthy-looking spreading mat of glossy green leaves, it seldom flowers freely—more often than not it doesn't flower at all. When the marvellous, trumpet-shaped blue flowers (2 inches long or more) do come thick together, then they are quite breath-taking in their beauty: there is nothing like them in the garden. This lovely Gentian needs an open sunny place, deep, light, loamy soil with plenty of limy grit in it, and may be propagated by division of the tufts as they grow bigger. Late June, as the flowers fade, is the best time. Keep the new little plants well watered. Press the soil round them very firmly and continue to do this till they are well established.

The autumn-blooming *G. sino-ornata* (Chinese form of the species *ornata*) has trumpet-flowers that come in autumn, often in late autumn. At the Savill Gardens in Windsor you will see a magnificent show about the middle of October. They are planted in wide drifts and fringe an open woodland. This species needs some shade and is a failure in full sun, though of course in late autumn the plants won't get much. More important than position however is the correct soil: it must be deep sandy moist leafmould free from any trace of lime. The flowers, funnel-shaped, about 2 inches long, are a deep glorious blue, pale near the base, and come at the tips of the stems which are creeping but erect at the ends; the leaves are narrow and bright green. The plants form rosettes and spread out into mats. Propagation is simply by division of the roots. The species is a native of Western China and Tibet.

There are at least another dozen rockery kinds offered by nurseries. They are all lovely and desirable and about as accommodating as one another—none very difficult, none very easy. I single out the hybrid *G.* × *macaulayi*, of garden origin, as the most popular. It is a cross between *G. Farreri* and *G. sino-ornata* and said to be easier in cultivation than either of its parents. The deep blue funnel-shaped trumpet flowers are 2½ inches long and come in autumn at the end of the stems. The plant needs a cool leafy soil (like *G. sino-ornata*) and eventually forms a spreading mat from which you can pull rooted pieces for new plants. These late-blooming Gentians are often in flower up to Christmas.

Gypsophilas are the extreme opposite of Gentians: they like lime and will thrive in full sun in dryish soils practically anywhere. First, for those people who have asked me: *Gypsophila* is pronounced with the accent on the *second* syllable: Gyp—*soph*—ila. There are about half a dozen species recommended for rockeries and the loveliest perhaps is *G. repens* (prostrate, creeping) and its varieties. My own choice is *Var. rosea*. It has been described by a grower as a 'Soft airy plant forming a cloud-like mass of tiny pretty pink flowers that will cover a rock or hang over one in midsummer'. A well-grown plant is a mound of branching growths, the 6-inch wiry stems carrying the tiny pink flowers (a third of an inch across) and grass-like, green leaves. The roots of *Gypsophila* go down deep, so a special place should be prepared for the plants. Our species comes from the Alps and is propagated by seed, cuttings or by division of the roots.

H

Haberlea are rare alpines from the Balkans. They are expensive: about 43p a plant. For that reason perhaps they are usually grown in an alpine house but according to specialists they are better outside in a rockery, if you can establish them there. Grow them as you do *Ramonda* (page 113). They need a crevice facing north where the soil is deep rich and leafy (use equal proportions of powdered peat or leafmould and sharp sand). *H. ferdinandi-coburgi* has large dark evergreen leaves (3 inches long) in rosettes and pale lilac-pink Gloxinia-like flowers (an inch long and an inch across—about four of them) on stems 4 inches tall. The plant was named in honour of King Ferdinand of Bulgaria, who was a student of alpine plants.

H. rhodopensis (of the Rhodope Mountain in Bulgaria) is a smaller plant with paler flowers. Both these choice alpines bloom in April. They are difficult to propagate (seed is difficult to get); when big enough they may be divided and planted in small pots and left till good strong roots have formed.

Helianthemum ('Rock Rose') are as common and easy as *Haberlea* are rare and difficult. Probably they are as frequently seen in our gardens as *Arabis, Aubrietia* and *Alyssum*. The garden varieties of *H. nummularium* (coin-like, circular) are the plants almost exclusively grown. Occasionally one comes across the species growing wild on our sunny hills; but its yellow flowers do not vie with those of the glorious golden-yellow and orange *Var. Ben Fhada* or with any of the other varieties—most nurseries list about twenty. These have flowers at least an inch across—twice the size of the wild ones—and some are double; there are white, pink, scarlet, brownish-orange shades and others, and good descriptions are given in nurserymen's catalogues. Like some of the shrub Rock-roses, *Cistus*, they get untidy after a season or two and should therefore be pruned or clipped over to keep them neat and tidy. Dead growths must be removed then, and at the same time cuttings of unflowered shoots may be taken and put to root in a sandy medium in a cold shady frame.

Helichrysum are the 'Everlastings' or 'Immortelles', the border varieties of which are hung up and dried for winter decoration. But the alpine kinds have small flowers, about ½ inch across; and they are mostly too fragile for exposure to our long damp winters. The few that are grown are usually treated as half-hardy plants and grown in the alpine house.

H. milfordinae, from Basutoland, South Africa, is said to be the most satisfactory for outdoors; but it needs a warm sheltered spot—a dry sunny shelf or ledge—in a rockery in a warm district. It forms a cushion of rosettes, with small pointed leaves covered with silver-white hairs; the daisy-like flowers, papery-white, stiff to the touch, have prominent yellow centres and come in June on short stems. Despite its reputed hardiness, the plant is best covered with a pane of glass from late autumn till the spring to protect it from excessive wet. It needs a well-drained light loamy soil. Propagate it by cuttings in late summer under glass.

Hepatica resemble Anemones and are often classed and described with them. They are useful to have in a rockery, since they bloom in late winter, when there isn't much to see. *H. triloba* (3-lobed) has blue, white, or pink flowers about ¾ inch wide, with yellow anthers, and heart-shaped, 3-lobed dark-green leaves. The plants like a semi-shady place and are excellent for providing patches of blue or pink near a flattish boulder or better still in the wild part of a large rock-garden where they can run and spread and be left undisturbed. Cool, moist, leafy soil is needed; and propagation is by seeds or by division when the plants have made big clumps, say, after three years.

Hypericum are the 'St. John's Worts' (*wort* is 'a plant or herb of any kind') and include the famous 'Rose of Sharon'. There are several species suitable for the rockery and the 'Rose of Sharon' (*H. calycinum*) is sometimes grown there, though it is too invasive for such a place and is best grown in the wild-garden where, by the way, it will flourish even under trees in deep shade. One of the choicest for the rock-garden is *H. coris* (*coris*: plant resembling a Thyme), with small golden-yellow flowers delicately streaked with red, and evergreen heather-like leaves. Its habit is shrubby—it's quite short: not above 9 inches; and the plant makes a neat mass of green when it finishes blooming in August. It comes from the mountains of Southern Europe and according to the R.H.S. Dictionary 'will not withstand severe frost'. It needs a sheltered place, then—and plenty of sun; and an open leafy moist soil and it is usually propagated from cuttings.

There are several charming kinds suitable for wall-gardens (Chapter 3).

I

Iberis are commonly known as 'Candytufts', though some gardeners reserve the name for the annual kinds that mostly have purplish flowers and are used for edging borders. The Alpine *Iberis* is an easy and favourite plant and takes its place with those other favourites, the *Arabis, Aubrietia, Alyssum* tribe. When in full bloom, it makes a mound of hard white flower-heads, a staring white in a mass; the plants may be grown on a low wall—where it is not so prominent (see page 108), especially if the spot is partially shady. This *Iberis* goes well with pink, purple or lavender, but quarrels with bright yellow, such as the yellow of *Alyssum saxatile*. *Iberis saxatile* and *I. sempervirens* and their varieties are the plants usually grown. They are evergreen and shrubby and spreading in habit and mostly like to be in high well-drained places. *I. sempervirens* is the bigger plant and attractive in winter with its small narrow evergreen leaves. These species come from the warm sunny slopes of the Southern European mountains and in cultivation need warm conditions and light, sandy, loamy soils; all are noted for their remarkable floriferousness. Propagate them from cuttings of small shoots in late summer.

Iris for the rock-garden are numerous. The best known and the easiest is *I. pumila* (low or small) and its varieties. The plants like a sunny place and deep loamy soil with lime in it. The leaves, sword-shaped and slightly glaucous are about 4 inches tall and come in tufts; if the plants are left undisturbed for some years, they will spread out into a mat of fleshy rhizomes covering the ground; it is an excellent little Iris for a pocket and will fill it with small purple-blue Flags packed tight together with no foliage visible, the same colour as the common purple-blue border Flag. The clumps need dividing about then and planting in fresh soil. No manure should be used. Unfortunately the flowers don't last long. April is their month. *Var. Azurea* is 'of neat habit with almost stemless blue flowers' says one nursery; *Cyanea* is pale blue; and *Lutea* is a form with yellow flowers. *I. pumila* is found wild in Southern Europe and Asia Minor.

There are several little bulbous species: *I. reticulata* (netted) is perhaps the best known and one of the most satisfactory for the rock-garden—some, especially the mid-winter-blooming species, are better housed under glass: *I. danfordiae*, yellow flowers in January, is one of these. Our plant, with roundish bulbs covered with a net-like coat, bears in March fragrant, deep-mauvish flowers with golden-yellow markings on the falls, and grows about 6 inches tall.* The leaves are narrow, rush-like; at first the same length as the flowers, then later very tall, up to 12 inches or

* Falls: those parts or petals of a flower which bend downward. O.E.D.

more. The varieties are more popular than the type. 'Cantab', with Cambridge-blue flowers marked with orange seems to be the favourite; and the red-purple 'Krelage', the best known. These Irises need a compost of equal parts of loam, leafmould and coarse sand; they should be set 3 inches deep, and 3 inches apart and planted in August or as soon as the bulbs are available. This species is a native of the Caucasus.

I. unguicularis (having a stalk or narrowed base to the petals) is a winter Iris that begins to show its buds in November and continues to bloom often till the spring—you might sometimes see the flowers as late as May. The rockery is a very good place for it, provided you have a good-sized vertical rock facing due south to grow it against; for it needs full hot sun to get it early in bloom and the sort of protection such a rock affords, if the flowers, which are very fragile, are to survive the winter. They are lilac and white with yellow markings and wonderfully fragrant, the scent reminiscent of Hyacinths. Plant this gem in poor, sandy lime-rubble soil, spreading out the fibrous roots flat in the soil; and do not disturb it. I think you can leave it in the same place for a lifetime. The leaves are untidy, long, narrow and rush-like. They may be shortened occasionally in August.

L

Leontopodium alpinum is the famous 'Edelweiss'—the word is German: literally 'noble-white'; though one could translate it as 'high-white'. It is a very common plant, often found in the lower regions of the Alps and not by any means rare as many people imagine. It is a true alpine. Its leaves are white and woolly—whiter, it is said, in poorish sandy soil—and its flowers, small and insignificant, come in clusters, and are enveloped in silvery-white larger bracts. Not really a striking plant, but useful as a foil to others that bloom when it is at its best—about June. (*Aster alpinus var. ruber*, with red flowers is a good choice.) The soil actually recommended for it is a firm, sandy one, with lime in it. You can raise it (and the alpine Asters) from seed, which is quite cheap to buy.

Linum alpinum: some collectors praise it; others dispraise it; Farrer calls it 'a weakly prostrate thing . . .' Hillier says 'An alpine gem. Flowers sky-blue. June—August'. (It costs about 25p.) It is 6 inches tall, with thin wiry stems carrying heather-like grey-green leaves and loose clusters of pale china-blue flowers; it is of tufted habit, spreading, and lovely to see in a pocket in full bloom during May and June. A native of the European Alps. *L. flavum* (nearly pure yellow), a taller plant, is often raised from seed: 5p a packet from Dobies' who call it 'A charming golden-yellow Flax suitable for the rock-garden or for borders. Hardy perennial. 1–1½ feet. July–August.' The popular name of *Linum* is 'Flax'.* *L. flavum* may be grown both in the rock-garden and in the herbaceous-border. Its flowers are yellow and come in branched heads or clusters, the leaves are narrow and bright green. This species is often grown in conjunction with the blue-flowered *L. perenne*, the species that grows wild in parts of Britain. The other is native to regions extending from Germany to Russia. Both are easily raised from seed and useful plants for a summer display and for providing contrast with low-growing alpines.

M

Meconopsis are Poppy-like plants (belonging like the genuine Poppies to the *Papaveraceae Family*). Two of the best known, to give them their popular names, are 'The Blue Poppy of Tibet' and 'The Welsh Poppy'. Neither however is indigenous only to the countries from which they get their names: the first is found in Yunnan and Upper Burma as well; the second fairly widely spread in Britain. The first is one of the aristocrats of the race; the other, the really plebeian member, seen in every garden and easy to grow practically anywhere—under trees in deep shade, on walls: put some seed on a brick wall and it will grow there! The best form is *Meconopsis cambrica var. aurantiaca flore pleno*, the double-flowered brilliant orange 'Welsh Poppy', brilliant and beautiful enough to be grown in a mass in the rock-gardens at

* Varieties of *Linum usitatissimum*, the Common European Flax, are especially grown for fibre for the making of linen.

Windsor Castle, as already mentioned (page 28). The brilliance of the colour is quite startling when seen for the first time. The type is yellow flowered; the leaves, deeply divided and rough or hairy; the plant is about 18 inches tall. It is very well known. I think it likes shade best; at least the flowers (1½ inches wide) seem to last longer than they do in full sun. The plant is propagated by seed. It is not recommended, by the way, by everybody for the rock-garden, because it seeds itself everywhere and is difficult to get rid of.

'The Blue Poppy' is *M. betonicifolia* (having leaves like those of *Betonica*), and is the species every gardener aspires to grow, but it is not a true rockery plant. In the wild it grows tall—up to 4 or 5 feet: in cultivation it is smaller. The best specimens I once saw in a rock-garden, however, growing in a specially prepared pocket in a shady spot. They grew in equal parts of sifted leaf-mould and coarse sand, in a place sheltered from wind and the hot midday sun. The flowers, 2 inches across, were a beautiful shade of sky-blue. This species is mostly raised from seed. Dobies' supply it at 5p a packet. 'Glorious sky-blue flowers with a central mass of golden anthers. A superb plant for a moist and partially shaded position.' Feed this species with a good artificial fertilizer from April onwards and you'll get magnificent big blue flowers and strong, truly perennial plants. Several *Meconopsis* have been recommended for the large rock-garden—*M. grandis* (blue), and the variety 'Branklyn', with Gentian blue flowers (expensive: £1·05 a plant); *M. integrifolia* (primrose-yellow); *M. latifolia* (pale blue); *M. punicea* (red); *M. quintuplinervia* (pale purple); *M. simplicifolia* (sky blue or purple); *M. villosa* (buttercup yellow). These species cost about 25p a plant. All may be raised from seed.

Mesembryanthemum are succulent plants from hot sunny countries and in Britain prosper only in warm gardens near the sea. If you garden, say, along the south coast, you can grow *M. edule* a trailer, on your walls, and *M. uncinatum* in the rockery. (Both cost about 50p each.) They are natives of South Africa and have attractive daisy-like flowers that usually open at midday. *M. uncinatum* is a shrubby plant with pink flowers ¾ inch across and grey-green leaves on prostrate stems that will flop over a sunny rock. It is easily raised from seed.

Muehlenbeckia axillaris is known as the 'Wire Plant' on account of its thin, thread-like stems. It is a slow growing, creeping shrublet, at first a couple of inches or so high, then developing into a mass of growths up to a height of about 12 inches. Having little or no floral beauty, it is often used as a contrasting plant, grown at the foot of a boulder on which some striking flowering plant is poised—one of the Euphorbias with some of its stems hanging over—or down which a purple Aubrietia is trailing. The plant is a native of New Zealand, Australia and Tasmania; its specific epithet refers to the tiny, greenish flowers growing in the axils (joints or angles formed by leaf and stem); the leaves are deciduous, the largest ½ inch long. Ordinary loamy soil is best for this rock shrublet. It is propagated from cuttings.

Myosotis are the 'Forget-me-nots' and those we grow as rock-plants are best in the Moraine. The species from New Zealand have white or yellow flowers: the lovely blue ones come from Europe.

O

Omphalodes are known as 'Creeping Forget-me-nots' and a few are suitable for the rockery. *O. verna* (vernal, appearing in spring) has intense blue flowers, with a white throat; they begin to show colour in March and continue in bloom till May, though the plant doesn't make a splash of colour as do the blue Gentians. It is about 6 inches high; the leaves, 1 to 3 inches long, are ovalish, with longish stems, and come in stolons, trailing or creeping along the ground; and the flowers, ½ inch wide, are borne in loose clusters and lovely in spring when they spread over the soil. This species, from the Southern Alps, likes cool shady places and leafy moist soil. Propagation is by division or by seed. The plant is familiarly known to collectors as 'Blue-eyed Mary': Mary, it is said, was Marie Antoinette, the fourth daughter of Maria Theresa of Austria, and the story is that she brought the plant to France with her when she married Louis XVI.

Onosma tauricum is the 'Gold Drop' plant from the warm regions of South-East Europe. Although it has this name, the plant is not known at all well; and it and the species *O.*

albo-pilosum are about the only two offered by nurseries. *O. tauricum* is recommended for a warm, sunny shelf in the rock-garden and also for a crevice in a wall facing south. The leaves, grey-green, are narrow and bristly hairy; the flowers, a clear golden yellow, hang in tubular waxen-like drops from the top of the 6-inch stems and are almond scented. *Onosmas* like a rich or fairly rich sandy loam and are often propagated by cuttings put in a closed frame. The specific epithet *tauricum* means 'of the Crimea', whose ancient name was Taurica Chersonese.

Ourisia coccinea (scarlet) is a choice, quite rare, alpine from the mountains of Chile. It is described by nurseries as having 'gorgeous scarlet, tubular flowers'. It costs about 38p, which is dearer than most rockery plants, these costing 25p or a little less. This species, like the others, makes a carpet of leaves that grow from the creeping rhizomes. It has rosettes of glossy, bright green, crinkled leaves, ovalish in shape; from their centre rise the very beautiful, scarlet, trumpet-shaped, drooping flowers (about 1½ inches long) in tiers on stems from 6 to 12 inches high. The plant makes a magnificent show of brilliant colour during the summer months, especially when half a dozen or more are grown in a mass. *O. coccinea* needs protection from the full heat of the sun, and likes a moist, rich, well-drained loam. It's a plant that needs care and attention; if you haven't a natural shady spot for it, you should put over it an artificial screen of some sort during the hottest part of the day.

Oxalis are the 'Wood Sorrels' or 'Shamrocks'; and the wood or the woodland is a good place for many of them—there are about 800 species, by the way. Nurseries offer usually six that are suitable for the rockery: one or two are best planted in the spring. *O. adenophylla* (with glandular leaves) from the Andes in Chile is one of these. Like the others, it needs a leafy, sandy, lightish soil and a dry warm position. It might be on the tender side in cold districts and then would be better housed; anyhow, it flourishes more luxuriantly in a sheltered nook. The finest specimen I ever saw grew in a cavity scooped out of a piece of tufa; the bulbous root was planted in loamy soil that was at least 7 inches deep; and the plant grew and prospered there for years. The flowers are lilac-pink, bell-shaped, an inch long and come singly on 3-inch stems from the centre of the bulb-stock; the leaves surrounding them are grey-green and divided like those of the 'Shamrock'. A beautiful plant that is best propagated by offsets. Like the spring bulbs, it disappears in winter.

Oxalis enneaphylla (leaves with nine divisions) has finely-divided leaves (Shamrock shape) of an attractive grey-green colour and fragrant white flowers an inch across on stems 2 or 3 inches tall. They bloom in early summer and like shade on them during midday. The soil must be deep, leafy, cool and moisture-retentive. The bulb-like rhizomes are best planted in autumn; mature ones may be divided then or offsets taken. This species is found wild in the Falkland Islands. The variety 'Rosea' seems to be better known to many gardeners. It has pretty, pink flowers and was given by the R.H.S. an Award of Merit in 1912. Both plants are sometimes grown in the alpine house especially in districts that get a lot of wet.

The specific name *Oxalis floribunda* is used for several species; but nurseries list it and describe the plant as having rose-coloured flowers carried well above the light green foliage and blooming in spring and summer. Suitable for the rockery or for a wall.

P

Papaver are Poppies, the best known of which are those grown in the herbaceous border, such as the Oriental Poppies (*Papaver orientale*), and the Iceland (*P. nudicaule*). The one recommended for the rockery is *P. alpinum*, with white flowers about an inch wide and its varieties now obtainable in shades of yellow, orange and pink. *P. nudicaule* is also used occasionally, though it is rather tall for the average rock-garden. *P. alpinum*, a true alpine, found on the higher slopes of the Carpathians in Central Europe and on the Southern Alps is often raised from seed—sown where the plants are to bloom. A packet costs 4p. You can buy good plants of course; they cost 15p each. These Poppies bloom all through the summer. The leaves, glaucous and finely divided, rather fern-like, and from 2 to 8 inches long, form a basal tuft from which rise the thin stems, 4 to 10 inches high, each carrying a flower often, in the varieties, 2 inches across. These dainty Alpine Poppies like a lightish, sandy loam and plenty of sun. They are not so prolific as the 'Welsh Poppy' (*Meconopsis cambrica*); they usually seed themselves round about where they grow, but you won't, I think, find seedlings settling on your brick walls and your pathways.

Occasionally one comes across *Papaver triniifolium*, a species from Asia Minor and noted for its curiously beautiful silvery glaucous foliage. (I can't, by the way, find the plant listed in any current catalogue.) It is biennial: seeds are sown in July (or earlier) and the plants raised are put out in October; they then make good strong growth, stand through the winter and are ready to flower the following season; after flowering they are finished and fresh seed must be sown for new plants. Before the flowers of *Papaver triniifolium* appear, the finely divided leaves on their long conspicuous stems spread out into a flat rosette that has a sculptural quality about it; the exactness of the design is quite beautiful—the flowers are small (on 12-inch stems) and a washy red. The plant grows well in any lightish loamy soil.

Penstemon are regarded by most people as border plants; and no doubt the reader has grown some of these from seed: the so-called 'Giant Hybrids' which are half-hardy perennials and raised annually. 'A magnificent large-flowered strain with large trumpet-shaped blooms of white, pink, deep rose and crimson, some having white throats.' A packet costs 4p from Dobies'. Dobies', by the way, spell the word *Pent-stemon* (which was fairly common in the past); but the spelling with one 't' now seems to prevail. The 'trumpet-shaped' or tubular-shaped blooms, with their prominent lips or lobes, are similar in all the *Penstemon*—they are often called Snapdragon Blooms. One of the best species for the rockery (not usually above 9 inches high) is *P. fruticosus* (bushy) from the Rocky Mountains of North-West America. If it grows well, it will in time make a wide-spreading mat of narrow leaves and purple flowers in late summer. It needs a sunny place. The variety *crassifolius*, with entire (undivided) leaves, is offered by many nurseries instead of the type. *P. menziesii* is like it; so too is *P. scouleri*, which forms large prostrate clumps of deep green leaves covered in summer with clusters of rose-purple flowers with a prominent lip. There is a beautiful white form called *Var. albus* and also *Var. roseus*, with rose-pink flowers. *P. newberryi* is noted for its scarlet-coloured flowers, which are borne very freely in June. The leaves, a good contrasting green, are ovalish and toothed; and the plant does best in partial shade. *Penstemon* are propagated by seed and by cuttings taken in August and rooted in a cold frame.

On the whole, they are rare plants.

Phlox are creeping or mat-forming alpines which many people like to grow on their wall-gardens. And they trail down very much like *Aubrietias* but often unfortunately succumb to damage by slugs and other pests and to winter wet and damp as well. I've lost many specimens of the lovely lilac-coloured *Phlox douglasii* after they have been growing well for a couple of years. This species is from Western North America (as are many of the rockery *Penstemons*) and need a cool leafy loam with plenty of sand or grit in it and always protection from winter wet, though it doesn't mind the cold. The plant is usually not more than 6 inches tall, the small stems with their five-petalled flowers growing in tufts and spreading out to form a close mat of lilac blossoms in May and June. The leaves are small and narrow ($\frac{1}{4}$ inch long) and are often quickly devoured by slugs. It is better grown on a shelf in the rockery, where you can put a cloche or something over it in the winter. It seems more difficult to protect on a wall.

Phlox subulata (awl-shaped leaves) has produced many charming varieties and it is these that are mostly grown in our rockeries. Slugs go for them and they are not as easy as *Aubrietia*, needing moisture during the summer and protection from too much wet in winter. They grow, like *P. douglasii*, tuftily, with stems from 2 to 6 inches tall; the leaves, about $\frac{1}{2}$ inch long, are awl-shaped (awl: a narrow steel piercer for making holes in leather), and the flowers, about $\frac{1}{2}$ inch across, come in clusters of 2 or 4. The variety *alba* is pure white, a beautiful plant; 'G. F. Wilson' is a popular cultivar* with almost blue flowers. 'Vivid' is a deep rose-pink. An old favourite. Lovely grown next to the sky-blue

---

* A cultivar is a variety of plant that has been produced only under cultivation. Thus 'Brilliant' is the cultivar name of *Sedum spectabile* 'Brilliant'; the specific name is *Sedum spectabile*.

77

Lithospermum diffusum 'Heavenly Blue', page 110. Alpine *Phlox* need a light clipping over after flowering to keep them neat. Propagate them by cuttings taken in late summer. Or you can root some of the stems by heaping a compost of sand and leaf-mould on to them and leaving them till roots have formed.

Polygonum are the 'Knotweeds'; and the species most widely grown in our rock-gardens is *P. affine*, a beautiful weed-like creeping plant that produces 9-inch spikes of tiny densely-packed pinkish flowers in September; there are several varieties and the best is 'Donald Lowndes', with shorter, thicker spikes of large rose-pink flowers. A valuable carpeter in the rockery for spreading over stones or along a rock-shelf. This variety was one of the plants collected in Nepal in 1950 by Colonel D. G. Lowndes. In mild districts the leaves, deep green and narrow, turn bronze in autumn and often remain through the winter till new growth commences. *Polygonum* succeed in ordinary loamy soil and are usually propagated by division. *P. affine* and its varieties are prized for their late show of flowers. They produce an enchanting effect associated with any of the purple Colchicums (so-called Autumn Crocuses). These Colchicums are strong-growing flowers, as tall as the *Polygonum* and will force their way up through the tangled growth of leaves and stems of the carpeting plant. But do not grow plants like the autumn-blooming Gentians (*Gentiana sino-ornata* for instance) near it, or they will probably be smothered. They should be planted in a pocket above the Polygonum: sky-blue above rose-pink.

Potentilla belong to the Strawberry family (*Rosaceae*) and have flat Strawberry-like flowers. The loveliest for alpine gardeners is *P. nitida* but it must be grown in the scree (page 127). And *P. verna var. nana* is also a special sort of plant: a miniature and best grown in a sink- or trough-garden (page 147); there are at least another half a dozen alpine kinds and *Potentilla alchemilloides* (like an *Alchemilla*) is singled out by nurseries as one of the most desirable. It grows up to 12 inches high and has long-stemmed, deeply-lobed or palmate leaves, dark green above and velvety white beneath; the flowers are pure white, an inch or more across, and come in flat compact clusters; they bloom practically all the summer. Grow it in a well-drained loam, in a sunny place; you may propagate it from cuttings taken in August.

Primulas, as most gardeners know, need some shade and usually a cool moist open soil if they are to prosper. Some that have grown from self-sown seed succeed in heavy, almost clayey soil but the plants are always protected from the direct rays of the sun. Polyanthus, a garden Primula (a cross between the native Primrose, *P. vulgaris* and the Cowslip, *P. veris*), doesn't mind clay; I've seen them growing sturdily from seed they shed two summers previously. These two aboriginal Primulas will often be seen flowering well in open fields, high up on hills or down by a river; and often you cannot dig them up with the roots intact if you try, for the ground is nearly always too hard; and it's probably the damp or dewy grass around them that keeps them thriving. They aren't grown much in the rockery: the open woodland is the ideal place for them. Some varieties of Primroses are, though: especially the coloured ones that you can raise cheaply from seed—sow it in the crevices where the plants are to bloom. The so-called Blue Flowered varieties (8p a packet) in colours ranging from pale lavender to deep blue, bloom from March to May. The common Primrose goes well with any of these; and it likes a fairly heavy loamy soil or soil in very good heart but not the sandy loams many alpine plants need. Primroses like semi-shade but not deep shade.

The Double Primroses are rare and more difficult. They need a richer, stiffer loam and plenty of feeding with weak liquid manure as they come into flower. Try them at the foot of a boulder. They are expensive: about 40p a plant. 'Our Pat' has deep lilac double flowers; *Lilacina plena* is a lighter shade of lilac; and *Alba plena* a double white. They need carefully dividing about every third year.

The Auriculas grown in the rockery are usually described as forms of *Primula × pubescens* (covered with soft hair or down); they are called Alpine Auriculas but often appear as front rank plants in the herbaceous border, where they do well as a rule. The genuine (true alpine) *Primula auricula*, common in the European Alps, has yellow, scented flowers and attractive fleshy evergreen leaves, dusted with farina (a white powdery substance); it is a difficult plant to grow. Nurseries offer several Auricula varieties

79

such as the yellow 'Celtic King' (30p a plant). 'Jean Walker': 'Mauve with cream eye, large and fragrant; a vigorous grower.' (25p). 'Old Dusty Miller': 'White farinose leaves and richly-scented yellow flowers. An old favourite.' (35p). You can how-ever get seed of many charming varieties quite cheaply. Sow it in cool semi-shady crevices as you do the Primrose seed. Accord-ing to a Primula specialist: 'Auriculas may be planted in deep crevices between rocks. Use a compost made of a mixture of peat, sand and loam, or leafmould instead of the peat. The roots should be tightly wedged between two stones. Use clay instead of loam to wedge the plants in, because it will hold moisture longer . . .' This method might be used for planting practically any of the Primulas that are grown in crevices in our rockeries. *P. allionii*, from the French and the Italian Maritime Alps, is one of these; it is, by the way, reputed to be the most difficult Primula in cultivation. It has inch-wide flowers, rose-pink, mauve or white, on 2-inch stems. It may be planted in a crevice in lime-stone rock and just enough clay should be used to keep the roots firmly in position; fill up with equal parts of sifted leafmould and coarse sand; water occasionally during a long hot dry spell. In the wild it makes sheets of blossom in March and April, the deep pink varieties giving a specially beautiful warm glow of colour high up in the Alps. It is a good test Primula or, indeed, plant: if you can grow it, you can grow anything. Most Primula enthusi-asts prefer to house it under glass, giving it a pan of specially made-up soil and almost daily attention. There are others much easier. Among them *P. denticulata*, another spring flowerer. It comes from the Himalaya. It's well known, with its round heads of mauve flowers packed tight on the end of shortish stems that arise from rosettes of farinose, ovalish leaves. A sturdy plant; it likes a heavyish loam and partial shade. Red and white flowered forms are obtainable from nurseries. And seed costs 5p a packet. The popular name is the 'Drumstick Primula'.

The more difficult species such as *P. farinosa; P. forrestii* (which too often succumbs to winter wet); *P. gracilipes* (and *P. boothii*, which is very much like it); and *P. nutans*, very beautiful but not long-lived in cultivation, all these, and others, are perhaps best housed in the alpine house. There are however several species as lovely and much easier: *P. rosea*, for instance, with clusters of bell-shaped rose-pink flowers with a yellow eye; or better still, the variety called 'Delight', which has rich rose-crimson flowers on short stems; both should be grown in damp soil, best near water, say, by the side of a rockery pool (page 177). Another is *P. juliae*, which forms a mat of roundish leaves from which arise the bright purple flowers on 2-inch stems. It blooms early and needs a cool position and soil that doesn't dry out in summer— very easy to propagate by division. 'Wanda' is a hybrid of *P. juliae* and better known than that species; it is an early bloomer, with claret-crimson flowers on 3-inch stems. Cool, moist soil again, and also for its companion varieties. 'E. R. Janes', with pinkish- orange flowers, is outstanding. If you can: grow this plant in a clump at the foot of a flattish boulder of Cotswold Rock, a bright cream stone; it shows up the pink-orange of the Primulas beauti- fully in midwinter.

Pulsatilla are known to most gardeners as Anemones and in some catalogues are still found under that name. (*Anemone pulsa- tilla* is the common plant, popularly called the 'Pasque Flower'),* but the correct name is *Pulsatilla vulgaris*. It is a native of Europe and grows wild in some parts of the U.K., usually on chalky downs. In cultivation the plant becomes taller—up to 8 or 10 inches high—and carries erect its open bell-shaped violet silky flowers in April above the feathery, hairy, fern-like foliage. A lovely plant for growing in clumps in a partially shady spot near a boulder. It likes a well drained loamy soil containing lime and should be left undisturbed. It is easily raised from seed. Nurseries offer 'Alba', a white-flowered plant, and various other kinds: some with red flowers. Pulsatillas are fine plants for the open woodland where they look doubly attractive grown with April- blooming Daffodils in the background.

R

Ramonda are described in the following chapter; they do best in a vertical crevice of a wall facing north.

---

* *Pasque*, an obsolete word for Easter. According to some writers the green dye that the plant produces was used in ancient times for staining Easter eggs.

Rhododendrons suitable for the rock-garden are the prostrate kinds that spread out mat-like and fill a good-sized pocket or grow in a specially made-up bed on rockwork, or on an artificial ledge, which is simply a cavity made in the rocks or stones to support the soil. And the soil, as already mentioned (page 22) must always be lime-free—a good peaty or leafy compost—equal parts of leafsoil mixed with washed, lime-free sand. And watering in dry weather must be done with rain-water. If you haven't any, use tap-water with the addition of the preparation 'Sequestrene', which is used primarily to correct iron deficiency in limy soils.

The alpine Roses of Europe (page 9) aren't so striking in bloom as the Asiatic species and the hybrids raised from them. 'Elizabeth' has already been mentioned (page 23). 'Creeping Jenny' (from the same stock), with large reddish bells, is more prostrate (it grows rather tall ultimately); 'Bluebird' has lovely violet-blue bells in April; another hybrid which grows taller in the course of years.

Of the species, I'd choose R. *imperator* (Emperor), with narrow funnel-shaped flowers of a pink-purple colour and narrow ovalish leaves; R. *radicans* (having rooting stems), with very beautiful purple flowers on single stems ½ inch long; and R. *camtschaticum* (of Kamtschatka, North-East Asia), with rose-crimson saucer-shaped flowers and fresh green leaves. All these shrublets bloom about May and, with the exception of the last-mentioned species, are evergreen. The plants need no pruning; but remove the flowers as soon as they have withered. These Rhododendrons are very slow growing plants and they cost about £1·05 each.

Rosa (roses) were mentioned in Chapter 1, page 27; and lovely though they are, they don't appeal to all rock-garden enthusiasts; many find it difficult to know exactly where to plant them. Quite recently I saw a group of the hybrid called 'Midget', 9 inches high, with tiny rose-red flowers and fern-like foliage, growing in a pocket low down in a sunny rock-garden, isolated from all creepers, trailers and mat-forming alpines; and there they looked rare and beautiful. Most of these miniatures have a long flowering season, usually from May to about October. They like a good deep loam on the heavy side, with a little lime in it, and should be pruned back in March—which is the best time for pruning roses.

S

Saxifraga is a genus of about 300 species, a huge family, which botanists have divided into sixteen or seventeen Groups or Sections. Nurseries prefer to have five or six only, the plants in these groups (species, varieties and hybrids) requiring more or less similar treatment in cultivation. Many offer roughly seventy different kinds. Few rockeries, including walls, moraines, rock pathways, etc., could accommodate all these. And of course one would need a volume in which to describe them all. I have chosen a few of the most popular, those that I've seen during the past season or two growing well in quite ordinary small rockeries in gardens around London.

Our first plant is 'London Pride'. It is, I suppose, the most popular of all the Saxifrages: seen everywhere and in practically any part of a garden: in herbaceous borders, along pathways, in rockeries and growing out of crevices in wall-gardens. Its name is *S. umbrosa* (shade-loving). It is very well known, with it's roundish, spoon-shaped leathery leaves in rosettes and its feathery, starry, rose-pink, spotted flowers on 10-inch stems which arise from the dark-green leaves. The plant spreads out into a mass and is easily propagated by division. The flowers you can cut for indoor decoration in June, and there is an extraordinary number of charming varieties. The type prefers partial shade; but the variegated forms full sun. They all thrive in open moist soils; chips and pebbles are usually sprinkled round the plants to help keep the soil moist and cool. 'London Pride' is a plant, it is said, that you never buy, for the simple reason that you can get a root from your neighbour who is sure to have it. This species is found in many parts of the world and occurs in Britain. Nurseries put the 'London Pride' Saxifrages in the Section headed VARIOUS, a miscellaneous collection of species, varieties and hybrids.

The Section containing some of the easiest plants is the one nurseries call MOSSY. Their rampant growth is perhaps a drawback to planting them in the small rockery. They can however be checked by carefully pulling up the pieces which are encroaching on other more valuable things. The varieties and hybrids of

S. moschata (musky) are all charming plants with their spreading mats of bright-green foliage and tiny flowers ¼ inch wide which spring up on 3-inch, or longer, stems. 'Peter Pan' is one of the finest, with deep pink flowers, with a white centre. 'Pixie', 3 inches tall, has dense, very compact foliage and tiny rose-red flowers. 'Winston Churchill' is larger, with large clear pink flowers on 6-inch stems; and the hybrid *S.* × *sanguinea superba* is another comparatively tall plant with good true crimson flowers. All these Mossy Saxifrages prosper in open, gritty soils and revel in moist shady places, but not dry shady places. After some years the clumps of foliage often show patches of brown in the middle; then it is time to divide the plants up and take the healthy rooted pieces for new stock.

S. aizoon (always alive) is one of the ENCRUSTED Saxifrages. These plants have rosettes of stiffish leaves encrusted with silver or a limy deposit, and send up graceful sprays of white, pink or pale yellow flowers. They are easy to grow in a sunny rockery and like a deep, gritty, limy soil. Excellent plants too for dry walls (Chapter 3). Our species, which blooms in early spring, is a native of Europe and North America, and is seemingly more adaptable than most, since it prospers well in partial shade and in practically any sort of garden soil, with or without lime. (It is the sort of plant one is always on the look out for.) The flower stems come erect, up to 12 inches high, and bear loose clusters of white flowers, often spotted with purple; the rosettes of white-edged leaves spread and form good-sized mats of foliage in time. These rosettes, or their off-sets, are easily separated to form new plants. The varieties and hybrids are numerous and very well known. I single out as especially attractive the following three: 'Balcana', 6 inches high, with large white flowers heavily spotted with red; 'Lutea', with large soft yellow flowers; and 'Rosea' which has clear rose flowers on stems about 10 inches high; its colour fades however in strong sunlight.

Perhaps the most famous of the Encrusted type is the plant known as 'Tumbling Waters', a hybrid between *S. lingulata* × *S. longifolia*. It is a magnificent Saxifrage, with tall massive plumes of snow-white blossoms (the spikes often 3 feet long), which arch out sideways and are most arresting in a mass, or individually. It is best above a big, sloping boulder. Plant it in a deep crevice where it can root well and show the beauty of its shape and flowers to perfection. The large rosettes, encrusted with silver, die after the flowering season, but off-sets will be found growing round them and these will provide the new plants. 'Southside Seedling', with branching stems carrying white blossoms spotted with dark crimson, is another delightful variety. These two Saxifrages cost about 40p each, nearly twice as much as the others.

The Sections, *Kabschia and Engleria,* are included under that single heading by most nurserymen. According to collectors, these Sections contain most of the 'jewels of the family'. The plants need more care and attention perhaps than many of the other Saxifrages and are therefore better off in pans and pots in the alpine house, at least, many experts prefer to grow them there.

The plants need both sun and moisture; but the sun must not be allowed to scorch the foliage during the summer: a position facing south-west is better, then, than one facing due south. Additional help is provided by planting them close against a rock, set several inches deep in the soil; the roots will naturally work downward and forage about for the moisture which collects round the base. Give them a compost of equal parts of leafy soil and sand and add lime-chips at the time of planting. Excessive winter rain will rot the cushion-like tufts of delicate foliage, so the plants should be protected by placing panes of glass over them during bad spells of weather. Of course, in the alpine house (see Chapter 5) you can control practically everything: temperature, moisture, amount of sun and shade; moreover your plants are safe from all harsh outdoor contingencies. The beautiful hybrid *S.* × *jenkinsae,* with blush-pink flowers, is best there—and dozens of others.

The popular outdoor Kabschia is the little hybrid *S.* × *apiculata* (terminated by a short but not stiff point: the leaves are so shaped). Its parentage is *S. marginata Rocheliana* × *S. sancta*—it was introduced in 1894 and is reputed to be the earliest hybrid of the Kabschia Section. An early flowerer, often in full bloom in February; and once well established, it grows down in wide-spreading mats of cushion rosettes over the rocks. Since it blooms so early, it would be safest among rocks facing north or north-west in a sheltered part of the rock-garden. During a bad frost, the frozen flowers have a chance of thawing out slowly, before the sun reaches them and damages them. The rosettes are small and emerald green in colour and from them rise up the clusters of tiny primrose-yellow flowers on 3-inch stems. The variety 'alba' is an exact counterpart except for its white flowers. Both are propagated by division in spring.

S. griesbachii is the most striking of the ENGLERIA Saxifrages and likes an open limy soil and a well drained position in the rockery, as do all those grown outdoors. The humped basal leaves encrusted with white are 3 inches across, and from them arise the arching 9-inch stems carrying the small pink flowers partially hidden by the calyxes (the calyx is the outer saucer-shaped part of a flower). The great attraction of this Saxifrage is its pre-dominating red colouring; the flowers bent over in a spike are pink and inconspicuous, and the calyxes and stem-leaves are densely covered with scarlet silky hairs, so red in fact that the plant seems to glow in the sun. Long exposure to heavy rains however rather spoils it. Maybe that is the reason why it is so often grown under glass. The best form is called 'Wisley Variety'; it has larger flower spikes and the red colouring is richer and more velvety. I recently saw both plants in a garden near Taplow, Bucks; they grew among smallish pieces of grey rock (the type called Essex Grey) which kept the situation moist and cool; the ground was also liberally sprinkled with limestone chippings. Both plants were increased by seed and reproduced successfully, since no other varieties—no other Saxifrages—were grown in that particular garden.

Sedums are as numerous as Saxifrages, but not so many are grown in our gardens and only about thirty different kinds are offered by nurseries—I have about three. Sedums are excellent plants, by the way, for growing on or in Tufa rock (pages 15 and 29), as are of course Saxifrages and Sempervivums, all commonly known as saxatile plants, many being found flourishing on rocks and stones in the wild.

On the whole Sedums lack the strong fascination that Saxi-frages have for us. Some, collectors say, are positively uninteresting. The flowers of the well-known border *Sedum spectabile* are a dusty pink, described as dowdy-looking by many people; the darker red forms are better and these plants (although tallish) are excellent for providing a splash of colour in large rockeries during October and November. Plant them in deep rich loam in a sunny place. Grey stone behind them will show up the flowers to advantage.

S. acre (sharp, generally referring to the taste) is the very common Stonecrop, which seems to grow anywhere. Not many gardeners like it and not many recommend it; it is certainly too invasive for the average rockery. But it can be controlled like many other things by simply pulling it up, or off places, where it is not wanted. The flowers are a good bright yellow, star-shaped, $\frac{1}{2}$ inch across; the leaves, slightly succulent, small, green, and bitter to the taste. The plant is found wild in the U.K., and is common in many parts of Europe and the Middle East. It blooms in summer.

S. spurium (many false names) is another useful mat-forming Sedum that grows well in poor soil and blooms conveniently late in the year. (It is a native of Northern Persia and the Caucasus.) The flowers, usually pink or crimson (occasionally white) are star-shaped, with dark centres and come in large clusters on erect reddish stems about 6 inches high. The leaves are green, roundish, about an inch long and slightly succulent; they form rosettes that spread rapidly. It is easily propagated by division. The form 'Schorbusser Blut' has bronze-tinted foliage and dark-red flowers. You can grow this Sedum and its varieties practically anywhere.

The one most of us prefer I think is *S. spathulifolium* (with spatula-shaped leaves), a native of Western North America, a Sedum prized for its rosettes of thick, fleshy grey-green leaves. When in bloom the yellow flower-heads unfortunately hide most of the foliage and the plant is less attractive then. The variety *purpureum* is the best form, with deep plum purple leaves covered with a heavy greyish bloom. If you grow the plant in a hot, dry crevice, the leaves turn red and are even more beautiful.

Through the autumn and the winter months charming mosaic-like effects can be obtained by planting various Sedums, noted for the beauty of their foliage, fairly close together on the edge of a rock and allowing them to cover it or partly cover it. *S. spathulifolium* will provide plum, purple, grey-white; *S. lydium*, bright red; *S. dasyphyllum*, grey-green; *S. acre*, light green and green tipped with yellow.

Two Sedums seldom seen on the rockery are *S.S. pilosum* and *sempervivoides*. Collectors have long extolled their beauties and advised would-be growers to plant them in pots in the alpine house, where they can be looked after better. The first (hairy) has rosettes covered with soft dense hairs and resembles a House-leek (*Sempervivum*); it is a biennial and not usually till the second year does it produce its short-stemmed, branching clusters of lovely rose-coloured flowers. After blooming, it dies but sets plenty of seed. Sow it in September under glass; this is the best way to have a stock of plants ready to grow on indoors or out-side. It does well enough in a light loamy open soil in a sheltered sunny place among the rocks and flowers in May and June.

The second also resembles a *Sempervivum* and is closely related to *S. pilosum*. It is likewise biennial, flowering in June and July, then dying and producing plenty of seed. The plant is a native of the Caucasus, where it is found growing on sunny ledges and in sheltered nooks among the rocks, and limy detritus, or debris washed down the slopes containing vegetable soil. The large, fleshy rosettes, metal green suffused with bronze, send up erect 6-inch stems with clusters of magnificent brilliant red flowers. Another aristocrat of the Sedum family and certainly well worth finding a place for in the alpine house.

Sempervivum are the 'Houseleeks', a genus according to botan-ists of twenty-five species, hardy fleshy rosette-plants, usually stemless, propagating themselves by means of young plants from the leaf axils. They are natives of the mountains of Central and Southern Europe.

The actual 'Houseleek' is *S. tectorum* (of roofs), naturalized in Britain but not indigenous to any part of the country. It is a very well known plant and appears on roofs and brick walls in some places; but not many people grow it in their rockeries. The rosette's leaves are usually tipped with purple, and the flowers, when they *do* appear, are purplish. There are hundreds of different varieties and hybrids. Quite a few, like *Var. triste*, with reddish-brown leaves and pink flowers, are worth growing in a pot for indoor decoration.

The next best known species is the 'Cobweb Houseleek', *S. arachnoideum* (cobwebby), found in rocky regions from the Pyrenees to the Carpathians. The 'cobwebs' are fine hairs connecting the tips of the leaves and the outstanding character of the plant: it is beautiful in winter and should be grown just for the sake of the foliage, the rosettes spreading and often covering big pieces of bare rock. The flowers are a pretty cherry-red or pink and come during the summer in clusters at the end of 3-inch erect stems. Like the genuine 'Houseleek', it has given innumerable hybrids and varieties both in nature and in cultivation. I haven't seen many of these, but *Var. tomentosum*, with larger rosettes which are reddish-coloured, appears in most catalogues. Attractive in a pot for indoors.

Sempervivums thrive in sandy soil containing plenty of rubble or brick dust; the larger grander ones need a richer loam. Use the offsets you find round the dead rosettes to increase your stock.

The tiniest ones, such as *S. octopodes*, are ideal plants for sink-gardens and troughs (Chapter 6).

Silene is as large a genus as *Sedum*, but only about half a dozen different species are listed in catalogues and these are all rockery-plants. Of these few, by far the best known and perhaps the most useful is *Silene schafta*. (In districts on the Caspian Sea the plant is simply known as *Schafta*.) You can raise it easily from seed. Dobies' advertise it at about 4p a packet: 'An extremely useful late-flowering rock or edging plant. Spreading tufts covered with rosy-purple flowers. Hardy Perennial. 6 inches. June-October.' It likes a light loamy soil and you can save your own seed if you wish and sow it in the spring. The leaves, a bright green, ovalish and pointed, come on 6-inch stems; and the sprays of brilliant rose-purple flowers form mats of colour for a long period when there is little else in bloom in the average rockery. This species is a native of the Caucasus.

Two other species we occasionally see in the rock-garden are *S. acaulis exscapa*, an inch high, with stemless pink flowers in May (it needs scree conditions); and *S. Hookeri*, from California, a rare lovely alpine with pale pink flowers (2 inches across) with cleft petals, each flower growing on a short stem arising from a tuft of grey hairy leaves. A choice plant liking scree conditions too, and moreover needing extra protection from cold and wet in the winter. Recommended for the alpine house.

The popular name of the Silenes is 'Catchfly'; they are so-called because of the sticky fluid found on the leaves, which entraps insects.

T

Thymus is one of those families containing alpines suitable for all sorts of places: there are varieties for the rockery proper; varieties for dry walls; some for the interstices of paving; yet others for the alpine lawn; and a beauty for a pan in the alpine house. The foliage of many has the characteristic thyme fragrance, reminiscent, a gardener says, of the sad scent of chrysanthemums.

The various forms of *Thymus drucei*, long-stemmed, creeping, mat-forming plants, are used both for covering flat boulders in the rockery and for trailing over walls and dry sunny banks. (They are often described under the name of *T. serphyllum*). The special favourite is *T. drucei* 'Coccineus', with rich crimson flowers and tiny dark green scented leaves, a creeping plant almost as common in our gardens as Aubrietia, but blooming later. There are many other forms: a delightful white-flowered one called 'Albus'; and a pink: 'Pink Chintz'. They all need a light, loamy soil in full sun. Divide them up in September or March for new stock or additional plants.

The hybrid *T* × *citriodorus*, a spreading dwarf bushlet is often grown for the sake of its lemon scent alone. *T. pseudolanuginosus* is the soft, pale grey-green hairy mat-thyme suitable for the alpine lawn; and *T. membranaceus*, a choice plant from Spain, does best in a pan in the alpine house.

V

Veronica is a large family of plants—small trees, shrubs, annual and perennial herbs—which many gardeners regard as on the tender side and needing winter protection. Some of the shrubby kinds from New Zealand certainly do best in southern maritime places; but most of the herbaceous rockery Veronicas are very hardy. *V. prostrata* is the favourite species, described by Hillier as 'A superb plant for rock-work, banks, steps, walling, etc.; June–August. 6 inches.' It is native to Europe and Northern Asia and has produced several very charming varieties; these Veronicas are invasive and best grown in large rockeries where they have plenty of room to spread. The type has small narrow ovalish leaves and dense racemes or spikes of bright blue flowers on erect stems. A lovely mat-forming plant for a sunny spot. It needs ordinary loamy soil and it is usually increased by division in March or August.

Of the varieties, I recommend 'Mrs. Holt', with pink flowers; 'Rosea', a deeper rose-pink; and 'Spode Blue', with exquisite pale China-blue flowers.

Viola is the family which includes the wonderfully fragrant Violets (raised from *Viola odorata*) and the popular Pansies, with their curiously attractive 'face' colourings. The alpine Viola that comes in for most praise is *V. gracilis* (slender); which is sometimes difficult to get, nurseries mostly offering the hybrid forms. These are perhaps not so elegant in appearance as the species itself, nor so graceful and slender. However, they are all beautiful plants and bloom on and off right through the summer months. *V. gracilis* itself has violet-purple velvet-like flowers, about an inch long on 4-inch stems and a mat of glossy green leaves. Nothing could be lovelier massed in a pocket in grey sandstone rock.

I suggest the following varieties for growing either in a pocket or on a wideish rock ledge, but not in a narrow crevice, where Violas always look out of place. 'Alba', pure white flowers; 'Golden Wave', rich gold; 'Lutea', deep yellow; 'Mrs. Samuel Pepys', lavender-blue, and very free flowering. These Violas have been given the group name of *V.* × *visseriana* and will be found under that name in catalogues.

The plants thrive in any well-drained soil, and may be propagated by cuttings in July or by careful division of the clumps in late September.

W

Wahlenbergia belong to the Family *Campanulaceae* and have bell-shaped flowers like the Campanulas and the bell-flowered race of *Edraianthus*, under which name many *Wahlenbergia* are now listed. The flowers in *Wahlenbergia* are often solitary: in *Edraianthus* they come in clusters. The New Zealand *W. albo-marginata* is the species usually grown in our rockeries. But more often than not—especially in gardens around London—I've seen it grown in its pot, sunk deep down in the soil; it is then lifted in late October and housed under glass till April. A choice bell-plant, with white flowers tinged with pale blue, borne singly on short stems that arise from tufts of spoon-shaped leaves about an inch long. Like all its race, it needs well-drained light gritty soil.

Two beauties are *W. pumilo* and *W. serpyllifolius* (from the Balkan Peninsula); both now called *Edraianthus*, and both best grown in the moraine, in good scree soil. (See Chapter 4.)

Z

Zauscheria is our last family. The plant we mostly see is *Z. californica*, though actually it is not at all common and like the *Wahlenbergia* not too robust in our winter weather. Its popular name is 'Californian Fuchsia'; it also has the delightful name of 'Humming Bird's Trumpet'. A native of California and Mexico, it is prized for its scarlet tubular flowers (an inch long) which come in loose sprays at the ends of the spreading branches, clothed with willow-like grey-green leaves. This shrubby plant is about 12 inches high, and blooms most conveniently in late summer and early autumn. An excellent wall-top plant and lovely and conspicuous growing on a ledge high up in the rockery. The soil must be light and leafy; never heavy. It is always advisable to take cuttings: do this in September and root them in a greenhouse or in a closed frame.

Of all the different kinds of alpines described in this chapter, probably not more than about twenty are commonly grown in our gardens. And those chosen are indubitably the easiest; they grow well in the rockery or perhaps on a dry wall. The more difficult often need moraine conditions; and the most difficult the alpine house.

CHAPTER 3

Wall-Gardens

A wall-garden is a retaining wall, that is, a wall built mostly of oblongish blocks of rock or stone (not bricks or cement) against an earth bank. And it is actually part of the bank, since the rocks or pieces of stone are embedded in the soil and help to support it. Planting is often done simultaneously with the building. And since the wall is a garden feature, it is built slanting backward a little from the base so that the plants in flower can be better displayed; imagine it quite upright covered with flowering trailers (or any other suitable plants), and you will agree that the effect would be top-heavy; less restful to the eye than the slightly receding wall.

'A delightful feature,' you might think, 'but only possible where you have a natural earth bank.' True; and there is no substitute: you can't, for instance, heap soil up in a certain spot and *make* a bank and build your wall against it; for in a very short time all the moisture will drain away and the plants will suffer—most of them probably perish.

The ideal site—the only suitable one perhaps—is the slope; the house may be at the bottom, half-way up or at the top. A bank can be cut out anywhere; for behind is always the gently rising ground providing the necessary moisture, which seeps through from the soil above and thus keeps the plants in the crevices provided with a constant supply of moisture.

The alternative seems to be excavation: digging out soil to sink part of the garden and make a natural bank that way. It is how I made my own wall-garden. It's much more difficult, because you've got to get rid of the soil you excavate. You can spread it evenly round the top. And this is usually done when the wall is a low one, say, not more than 2 feet deep. A good plan is to have steps from the house leading down to a sunk area (say, 18 inches to 2 feet deep), the area being enclosed by the wall, which can be rectangular (three sides plus the side with the steps) or curved.

Choice of stone depends on the size of the wall, or more specifically, on its height. A 5-foot wall needs bigger pieces of stone or rock than the low 18-inch wall. For the latter: pieces as small as 12 inches long by 3 inches high may be used; as regards depth or thickness: experts say that the stones should be deeply embedded in the bank and recommend that at least 4 inches should be covered with soil.

Kentish Ragstone and Limestone and even Granite are often used for building wall-gardens. You can get what is known as Random Walling Stone from most rock-garden specialists. This is irregularly shaped stone, often small-sized and therefore not particularly good for rockeries. *Cheshire Lilac Random Square Walling*, 6 inches wide by 8 inches thick is favoured by many gardeners. These partly square blocks are excellent for the base of the wall and also for insetting higher up at intervals to strengthen the structure; though of course if the stone is well embedded in the soil, there should be no danger of its toppling—here and there, if you like, you can cement pieces in position. Another way is to lay some of the thinner pieces or slabs at right angles to the rest of the horizontally-laid stone. This will also strengthen the wall. (See pages 7 to 16 and footnote on page 16 for various kinds of stone.)

The stone should be attractive to look at; for not all the stone in a wall-garden will be covered with plants: if it were, one might just as well use an earth bank. Don't use, then, bricks or cement rubble from demolished buildings; for these crude materials will stand out conspicuously against the good stone and spoil the look of the wall.

Planting, as I've already mentioned, is often done as the wall is being built. On the other hand, many gardeners prefer to sow seeds in the crevices; it is the cheapest way, though of course much slower than buying well-rooted plants in pots.

From most seedsmen you can buy packets of *Arabis, Aubrietia, Alyssum, Campanula, Dianthus,* etc. These are described as 'Excellent for the rock-garden and for planting on dry rock walls'. 'Dry' is perhaps misleading; it doesn't mean 'parched' or 'desert-like'; but simply 'without mortar or cement'.

In a natural retaining wall, where the soil of the bank is reasonably good—loamy and leafy—sufficient moisture will be retained in the lower strata to satisfy plants like Primulas and Ferns. Here most of the moisture will be concentrated; and here therefore all the moisture-loving plants must be grown, provided of course the aspect is right. Some *Primulas*, for instance, need shade throughout the day as do practically all the Ferns. And, with the exception of those desert plants like Cacti and similar things, the vast majority of wall plants prefer shade on them during hot sunny spells. The Campanulas' bells last longer in partial shade; exposed to full glaring sun, they soon begin to wilt and fade and the show is quickly over.

A good wall compost consists of equal parts of loam (get it from a well cultivated kitchen-garden), sifted leaf-soil from the woodland and washed or silver sand. You can add to or take away from any of these ingredients to suit the particular plants you are growing; more leaf-soil for the Primulas, Primroses and Auriculas and other moisture-loving alpines; less leaf-soil and more sand and rubble for succulent types of plants; and just ordinary garden loam for the more common *Arabis, Aubrietia, Alyssum*.

Seeds of most plants will germinate reasonably well in the compost.

Alpines from the nurseries come well rooted in small pots and are best planted as you put the stones in position. Normally the roots aren't dry; but if they should be, stand the pots up to their rims in water till they are thoroughly soaked through.

Spread the roots out when you put the plants in the place selected. And this must be the right one; rampant trailers and creepers must be grown at the top not at the bottom—where they can't possibly trail. So first study the character of the plant; trailers must trail; cushion-forming plants, like the House Leeks (*Sempervivum*) can go practically anywhere: they would make, in time, good solid-looking foundation plants along the bottom of a wall, rather like a skirting. Shrubby and tufty plants may be

Pulsatilla vernalis, an alpine that grows high up in the mountain snows. Best in the moraine.

Dianthus gratianopolitanus 'Baker's Variety' (page 163), a charming pink for a pathway or for steps in a rock garden.

Juniperus horizontalis procumbens, a rare or rarish flat evergreen shrub for the rockery or the Alpine Lawn.

Alpine Campanula or Bell-flower growing at the bottom of a rock.

An early flowering Saxifrage (*Bergenia ciliata*) providing pale red flowers in March.

Dryas octopetala, an Anemone-like flower; an "easy" flower for any rockery.

planted almost anywhere. The shrubs as a rule have powerful roots that may in the course of time dislodge some of the smaller stones. So use heavy pieces where you plant shrubs, or cement the stones in position.

There are plants, such as *Arenaria balearica*, that creep in all directions; they don't trail, but they get into all the crevices and will eventually cover most of the stone. Another, much less attractive, is *Sedum acre*, the common Stonecrop with tiny fleshy leaves and yellow flowers. You control them by simply removing what you don't want; pull off pieces where you want the bare wall to be visible. The *Arenaria*, however, is an enchanting little moss-like creeper, with minute, white, pin-head flowers and is always delightful to see. It won't thrive everywhere; for it must have shady moist stones to grow on and cover.

Pruning is simple enough: when the plants get too big, just cut them back (trailers); or pull the rooted pieces gently off the wall (some *Sedums* and *Sempervivums*, for instance). Certain plants, such as *Aubrietia* and the Creeping Rock Roses (*Helianthemums*) need drastic cutting. Others (the double White *Arabis* is one) should be treated more leniently; cut this back too far and too often and you will probably kill it in time.

There are plenty of suitable plants for retaining walls; most nurseries list about fifty. A good number have already been mentioned in the previous Chapter.

Aethionema are not common and the name 'Persian Candytuft' is not well known. Many of them come from the very warm regions of the Mediterranean and aren't particularly easy to grow in our gardens: certainly not in bleak cold places. *A. grandiflorum* and *A. pulchellum* are usually chosen for walls.

The first has spreading branches 18 inches long, with glaucous (bluish-green) tiny leaves and glowing rose-coloured Candytuft-like flowers in summer. Plant it toward the top of the wall or half-way down and let it face the warm south if you can. Take cuttings in late summer in case of losses. Root them in a frame or in a cool greenhouse.

A. pulchellum (pretty) is found on the Elburz, a lofty mountain range in Northern Persia. It has branched stems, the side shoots carrying tiny glaucous leaves and rose-lilac flowers, the latter coming in dense clusters in late spring. Indeed a pretty plant; it will thrive in a sunny crevice of a wall facing south: a charming alpine for a low wall, where it can trail effectively. The dwarf Brooms (*Genista*), which bear pea-shaped yellow flowers, make good companion plants; both *Aethionema* and *Genista* should be given plenty of room in which to spread. They can touch, but shouldn't smother each other. Keep them in place by judicious pruning after they have finished blooming. Both like sandy loam, the *Aethionema* should also be given a little leaf mould.

Alyssum ('Gold Dust'), described in the previous chapter, are fine wall trailers, although a fully-grown plant can be untidy looking on a low wall, soon swamping it and touching the ground. *A. saxatile var. citrinus*, is one of the most beautiful of several varieties and has lemon-yellow flowers which go well with the lavender-flowered *Aubrietia* called 'Lavender'—both good reliable wall plants, that do well in any ordinary garden soils. Seeds cost about 3p a packet. Both can easily be increased by cuttings. The *Alyssum* comes from the Alps of South-East Europe.

Androsace lanuginosa (woolly) was mentioned on page 46 as a silver-leaved trailer, with bunches of small pinkish-white flowers with a yellow eye. The leaves are woolly, silver-green and about ½ inch long. The plant trails delightfully from a wall crevice and is usually safe there from excessive winter rain, which so often damages the leaves, as it naturally does the woolly or hairy leaves of all the Androsaces. The variety 'Leichtlinii' has whitish flowers with a pink or a yellow eye. It was named in honour of Max Leichtlin, a German collector who introduced many rare plants into Europe.

These Androsaces come from the North-Western Himalayas and are valued for their late (August) show of flowers. A protruding rock in the wall would help to protect them during the winter months, though a sheet of glass placed at an angle against the wall would be almost as good. They are very hardy; they like the sun and need the usual gritty, scree soil as do all the other members of the *Chamaejasme* Section mentioned on page 46.

Antirrhinum asarina, when not in flower, is a greyish-white-looking plant; the leaves are ivy-shaped and small and from the stem joints come the 'Snapdragon' flowers, pale yellow in colour, touched with red and about 1½ inches long. They stand out well on their stems against the greyish leaves and have a longish season: from about June to September. The plant is more floriferous in light, limy soils than in heavy loam, which always encourages stronger growth of leaf and stem. The word *asarina* is a vernacular name of *Antirrhinum*. The plant is a native of the South of France and neither it nor the following species is as hardy as the two Androsaces just described. Plant them in spring and give them some winter protection: let them have a position facing south and stand sheets of glass over them during cold wet spells.

Antirrhinum glutinosum (sticky, gluey) is a glandular, hairy plant with fragile sticky branches that trail down a wall and carry small ovalish leaves and pale yellow flowers striped with red; they are borne on single stems. 'A colourless plant,' say some gardeners, 'and the pink varieties, especially "Roseum", with largish pink flowers, are much superior'. The species is found on rocky slopes in central Spain and it needs a warm, sheltered place in cultivation. A light, limy soil is best for these plants. They are propagated by cuttings or by seeds. You can, by the way, grow with them or around them in the crevices of the wall, the much more showy annual 'Tom Thumb' dwarf 'Snapdragons' by simply sowing the seed about July where the plants are to bloom the following year. There is a wide range of colours. Dobies, offer 'Magic Carpet', 6 inches tall: 'Dwarf trailing habit in many attractive colours, ideal for the rock-garden.' These are perfectly hardy but best raised every year.

Arabis is very often used as a buffer plant when *Aubrietia* and *Alyssum* are grown on a wall, its white flowers coming between the bright, rather hard, yellow of the *Alyssum* and the vivid reds or purples or lavenders of the *Aubrietia*. Thus there is no clashing of colours. The double variety *Arabis albida* (white) *flore pleno* is the one mostly grown, since it comes a little later than the single white that begins blooming often in late January, if it's mild. The single in time makes an enormous spreading mat of flowers on 6-inch stems and like *Cerastium tomentosum* (page 57) needs planting on a sunny bank on its own. White *Arabis*, by the way, is often called 'Snow in Summer' which popular name really belongs to the *Cerastium*: *Arabis* is correctly 'Rock Cress'. The Double White is less invasive and not so vigorous, nor is it so permanent as the single, consequently it is advisable to peg the stems down into the soil so that they root and eventually form new plants. This can only be done of course to the stems growing on the soil at the top of the wall.

The Double White flowers when in full bloom are reminiscent of Lilies of the Valley; and you will sometimes see the small blue *Chionodoxa sardensia* ('Glory of the Snow') planted in among the white flowers—a delightful association for March and the planting can be done on the wall-top.

There is a form with flowers slightly tinged pink; and also a single pink—*rosa-bella* of rather more compact growth than the single white; and *variegata* has leaves variegated with yellow. The leaves of all these *Arabis* have a curious, stuffy musty smell, but not really perceptible unless you bruise or finger the leaves.

Ordinary light loamy soil suits these plants; they like sun or partial shade and are easily propagated by cuttings of small unflowered shoots in late summer. Seed of the single pink variety can be got quite cheaply.

Arabis albida is a native of South-Eastern Europe and is found wild as far south as Persia.

Arenaria balearica, from the Balearic Islands, Corsica and other islands in the Mediterranean, is well known (I've mentioned it several times already); it creeps rapidly over rocks, paths or practically anything, provided the place is shady and moist. It is ideal for a damp, shady wall; if you like its tiny white star-flowers and deep green moss-like foliage, protect it during particularly severe winters, for it isn't all that hardy—you needn't worry much about its spreading too far; it might disappear altogether one day. Gritty, limy soil (scree-type) in a crevice to start it growing well.

I've seen it used in conjunction with *Double White Arabis* and *Aubrietia* 'Lavender' on a low wall, some 30 feet long, the plants growing down the wall, with a space of about a foot between them; *Arenaria, Aubrietia, Arabis*, repeated in that order to fill the wall. A very effective arrangement. *A. montana* (of the mountains) is one of the best of the family for a wall, but not seen much these days. It comes from the mountainous regions of France and of Spain, is completely hardy but sometimes has the habit of dying off; perhaps like some other alpines, it is not long-lived in cultivation. Its creeping stems carry small narrowish leaves and lovely big white single flowers that are flat and open in May and June and come on 3-inch stalks. It likes light, gritty, leafy soil and partial shade, it seems. It should be increased by seed and it might be advisable to sow some every year, say, in September when it is just ripe.

Artemisia we know are famous for their finely-cut, fern-like foliage. Many have small uninteresting yellow flowers; the foliage of some is pleasantly fragrant when bruised; and those that are dwarfish may be grown as decorative shrubs along the top of a wall. Our Southerwood (*Artemisia abrotanum*) is one; its leaves are pungently aromatic and the plant is attractive for at least six months of the year. Some species are more lax in form and inclined to flop or even trail when planted in a suitable position. *A. stelleriana* (page 52), with silvery-white, downy foliage is ideal for the top of a dry wall; plant it in light sandy soil and let it grow over the rock-face. This soft, white-downy-looking *Artemisia* makes an excellent foil-plant to trailers with pale pink or lavender flowers; try it with the 'Rock Rose' (Helianthemum), called 'Rhodanthe Carneum' which has pale pink flowers with an orange centre. *A. stelleriana* is a native of North-Eastern Asia and of Eastern North America. Propagate it by cuttings.

Aubrietia is so well known and so successful in gardens—and in most places in gardens—that writers find it difficult to discover anything new about it and its cultivation. First, however, the actual word; the original spelling was *Aubrieta*, and this word appears currently in many botanical works. But practically everybody speaks of *Aubrietia* and *Aubrietias*. The name commemorates the famous French botanical artist Claude Aubriet, 1686–1743. Aubrietias really like a rather richer, loamier soil than they usually get and after flowering should be cut back to within an inch or so of the base of the stems. Propagation is by cuttings in late summer (put the shoots in a cold frame to root—use light sandy soil) or by layering the stems in spring.

The varieties we grow are either selected seedlings of *A. deltoidea*, Sicily to Asia Minor, or hybrids between this species and several others from the warm regions of the Mediterranean. Plants seldom come true to colour from the seeds you sow. Seed, however, is plentiful and cheap; sow in a frame in spring and keep only the best true colours. Aubrietias succeed in sun or shade but must be kept away from the drip of trees. 'Doctor Mules' is still the best deep rich purple, probably the favourite variety; 'Lavender' has soft lavender flowers; and 'Barker's Double' pink double or semi-double flowers. At least another dozen will be found listed in catalogues.

'Calamints' (*Calamintha alpina*; and *C. grandiflora*, which is sometimes regarded as a variety of the former), with their Thyme-like fragrant flowers are often planted on a low dry sunny wall and grown there along with the more woody Helianthemums: good companion plants for them (see page 55).

Calandrinia umbellata, because it is inclined to disappear during wet winters, has been recommended for the alpine house or for a sheltered dry wall (page 55). It is often raised annually from seed and treated as a biennial. Its garish flowers, a magenta-crimson, give a bright show in full sun during early summer. The variety 'Amaranth' (vivid crimson-purple) is usually offered by nurseries.

Campanula do well on walls but really need more shade than the *Calandrinia*. The species usually chosen is the very hardy *C. portenschlagiana*, with light blue-purple bells that go well with the creeping miniature yellow Nasturtium. There are others as indestructible as this species, and many as attractive. *C. garganica* (from Mount Gargano, Southern Italy) is a strong, spreading, trailing plant, which soon covers a large patch of wall-face with its exquisite open, or flattish, bell-shaped flowers, blue or mauvish —the colour is variable—and ivy-shaped leaves. There are several varieties. These plants need a rich sandy loam and are best propagated every so often to ensure a good healthy stock.

Another beauty is *C. poscharskyana*, described as a magnified *C. garganica*; it has lavender-blue star-shaped flowers that bloom through the summer till the autumn. A valuable bellflower for a wall and preferring limy, sandy soils. The plant was named in honour of Gustav A. Poscharsky, a garden-inspector of Dresden.

One can also plant species like the large flowered *C. carpatica* (from the Carpathian Mountains) in crevices of loamy leafy soil. This Campanula will make delightful clumps of large open bell-shaped, lavender-blue flowers; in time the clumps touching one another take on the semblance of a trailing carpet of large bell-flowers. The miniature flowered Nasturtium (*Tropaeolum poly-phyllum*) is an ideal companion-plant for any of these bellflowers; if it is a failure—and it doesn't succeed in every garden—grow instead some of the Brooms, which are tougher plants; *Cytisus decumbers*, with yellow open flowers in June, is a good choice. Another plant is *Euphorbia myrsinites*, with its glaucous green foliage and yellow flowers in early summer (page 63).

Ceratostigma plumbaginoides ('Leadwort') and *Cistus* (shrub 'Rock Roses') are often grown along the top of a sunny wall; eventually they grow over the top and down the face of it and are then very conspicuous, especially the Cistuses when covered with big open flowers. Most shrubs have a tendency to do this, the branches following the general contour of the rock-work. In warm maritime parts you often see huge blue Hydrangeas growing over walls in this way. Shrubs are best used only on high walls.

Convolvulus, according to the nurserymen, are expensive and sometimes difficult to get. *C. cneorum* (*cneorum*; pronounced with a hard 'c') is a fine, rare-looking dwarf shrub for the top of a wall-garden; it has silvery silky, narrow, lance-shaped leaves and pale pink or white funnel-shaped flowers on short stems in May. A rather tender shrub; it needs full sun and winter protection as a rule. A favourite pot-plant, by the way. (*Cneorum* is a shrub resembling the Olive.) Our plant costs about 6op.

Convolvulus mauritanicus (of Morocco) is the favourite trailing species for a wall. The flowers, an inch across, blue-mauve and open with a white centre, bloom from June till mid-autumn; the leaves are roundish and grey-green in colour. The stems carrying flowers and leaves trail down 2 feet or more and grow strong and vigorous in a hot sunny place. The plant is a failure on shady walls and in cold exposed gardens. Propagation is usually by division of the roots in May or after the plant has flowered; let the rooted pieces grow on in pots under glass; divide only well grown mature plants. This species and the following like perfectly drained, light, loamy soil with a little leafmould in it.

C. tenuissimus (extremely thin or slender, referring probably to the divided leaves), a trailing species from Greece, needing plenty of sun and a warm sunny wall to trail down. It bears large, rose-pink flowers from April till midsummer; these come singly on short stems and stand out well against the finely-cut leaves which are of an attractive silver-grey colour. Both these *Convolvulus* are rare. In many catalogues they are listed but not priced.

Dianthus are ideal plants for growing on a wall, for many trail naturally and when not in flower provide a pleasing mass of blue-green foliage. I'm thinking especially of the 'Cheddar Pink', which is particularly useful to have on a wall where it might not be possible to have anything in flower through the winter months. Grow it in conjunction with *Sedum spathulifolium* 'Purpureum' which forms small rosettes of plum-coloured fleshy leaves that grow out into a flattish mat and are a delight during the long winter months. The 'Cheddar Pink's' flowers are scented; and I think most people prefer the scented kinds to the scentless.

D. sylvestris is a lovely wall Pink but unfortunately usually scentless; it comes from the Southern Alps where it is found growing on rocky banks, covering them with grass-green mats of foliage and rose-coloured flowers an inch or more across on short single stems. Grow it on a sunny wall and in a crevice of light gritty soil and let it spread and increase there. The word *sylvestris* literally means 'of a wood or forest'; but here it designates a plant growing wild, not cultivated: our plant is never found in woods or forests.

Many of the scented hybrids are delightful on a wall. They are useful plants, raised primarily as Border Pinks, but readily adapt themselves to pockets in rockeries and crevices in walls. They can be grown in the way that was suggested for *Campanula carpatica* (page 103). They need a rich loam and plenty of sun. The old favourite, pure white double 'Mrs Sinkins' does well in such a place—a Pink famous for its rich warm scent and long flowering period. Grow with it the clove-scented 'Dusky' with darkish pink double flowers.

A writer on rock-gardening once told me that the important hardy trailers for a wall could practically be counted on the fingers of one hand. They were, he said; *Aubrietia, Arabis, Alyssum, Dianthus* and *Helianthemum.* These can look after themselves: you plant them in ordinary soil and leave them, cutting them back when they get too big. Alpine catalogues give another forty-odd plants. Many however are difficult and better off grown in pans and pots in the alpine house. And not all are really good trailers.

Erigeron mucronatus and *Erinus alpinus* are recommended. Apparently they aren't known to many gardeners. The first has small aster- or daisy-like flowers, white above and pinkish-mauve beneath, with yellow centres, the flowers carried on thin 6-inch stems; the leaves lance-shaped (*mucronatus*—terminated by a sharp point). A most floriferous plant, spreading wide and far by underground stems in a place that suits it. It needs a light, loamy soil in a crevice at the top of a warm sunny wall and prospers well probably only in southern districts. A native of Mexico and liable to perish during a bad winter. Cuttings should be taken in autumn and housed in a cold frame.

Erinus alpinus, a native of the mountains of Western Europe, and naturalized in some parts of Britain, has produced several varieties, the best of which is said to be 'Dr. Haenaele' with carmine-coloured flowers; the type, with white flowers, looks more attractive when set next to it. *Erinus* are tufted plants, with small oblongish, hairy leaves and racemes or clusters of flowers on 4-inch stems, blooming during May and June. A friend of mine who grows it says: 'It looks best trailing down a crevice between the rocks of a wall and should be planted in gritty, sandy soil.' It isn't usually long-lived and therefore should be raised annually from seeds sown in May in a frame. The Erinuses belong to the 'Snapdragon' family and the popular name is 'Fairy Foxglove'. The variety *carmineus*, with reddish flowers is more striking than the white one: '*albus.*'

Ferns and *Festuca* (the dwarf ornamental blue-green grass) are recommended for dry walls.

The species of ferns chosen must be hardy of course and they must be planted in shady, moist places and sheltered from high winds. 'Dry walls' sound inimical to them to say the least; but walls facing due north are all right: there are quite a number of species that may be grown in crevices low down on these walls and will prosper and serve as a foil to shade-loving alpines such as *Ramonda* and some of the Primulas.

It is best to choose small ferns, because the large kinds—those that grow very big—would ultimately hide the things associated with them. Try the evergreen *Asplenium adiantum-nigrum*, the 'Black Spleenwort', which is about 9 inches tall and has beautifully divided foliage, dark and leathery above and brown and soft with spore masses beneath. It is almost cosmopolitan; you will find it in some parts of Britain. It needs a compost of equal parts of leafmould, sandy loam, lime rubble and coarse peat. Propagation is by division in spring. Grow in a crevice next to it, if you can, the lilac-blue-flowered *Ramonda myconi*. They go very well together.

Much smaller is *Asplenium ruta-muraria*, with dark green divided leaves. Lovely associated with Double Primroses, if you can grow these, or with the single coloured ones which are very easy in shady crevices. This tiny fern likes limy rubble to grow in but should be started off in a little loam.

The easiest hardy fern is probably the evergreen 'Hart's Tongue' (*Phyllitis scolopendium*) another native; and very well known with its strap-shaped fronds, striped with brown spore masses beneath. It is one of the toughest of hardy ferns and will even thrive in sun, provided the soil is kept moist. Plant it in sandy leafmould and water it on hot days—when the sun has gone down. Propagation is usually by division of the crowns. These ferns cost about 30p each.

More expensive and rarer is *Polystichum setigerum var. Plumoso-divisilobum*; it has very finely cut, feathery-looking fronds that are a perfect foil to any alpine you grow near it. Once established in deep, moisture retaining peat-loam, it will tolerate strong sunlight. It costs about 75p.

Festuca, the blue-green ornamental grass, is a very adaptable plant but flourishes more luxuriantly in sun than in shade and in deep loamy sandy soil, not rich soil. You may grow it, if you wish, on a shady wall and have a clump or two in a crevice next to one of the ferns I have just described. You get not much colour but a fine contrast in foliage. Divide this ornamental grass every third year if you want the best strong-growing plants. It is a tufted plant, about 9 inches tall, and produces its flowers (grass spikes), purplish in colour, in summer. I think the rock Irises are about the most suitable things that you can grow along with it on a wall-top. The form most of us grow is *Festuca ovina glauca* (*ovina* means: of sheep or sought by sheep).

Helianthemum is one of the indispensable hardy trailers for a wall. The trailing rock-roses are so well known that it seems a waste of time to say much about them now. They seem to grow anywhere and in any ordinary garden soil, as mentioned on page 67. All that need be said here is that they should be planted at the top of a wall and allowed to spread out and trail down it; their long shrubby or perennial woody stems should be cut back after a year or two to promote fresh strong growth.

A charming and ideal companion for any of these Helianthe-mums is *Gypsophila repens var. rosea* described on page 66. It makes a delicate fairy cloud of tiny pink flowers, reminiscent of the larger white border *Gypsophila*. Since this alpine needs a deep root run, it would be a good idea to plant it when the wall is being built.

Next we come to a truly rare alpine recommended for wall crevices; this is *Helichrysum bellidioides* (resembling a daisy) a creeping, trailing 'Everlasting' with white daisy-like flower-heads $\frac{1}{2}$ inch across on erect, short slender stalks; the leaves are ovalish, about $\frac{1}{4}$ inch long, and silvery-white and woolly. A choice trailer from New Zealand but unfortunately only half hardy in our gardens. It is apt to die back and disappear quite often. So give it a warm, sheltered crevice on a wall facing south in a sheltered garden and always protect it with glass during a prolonged spell of wet. It needs a light loamy soil, perfectly drained and should be increased by cuttings taken in September and housed and rooted under glass.

Grow with this *Helichrysum*, the 'Rock Soapwort' *Saponaria ocymoides* (resembling *Ocymun* or *Ocimum*); which is a loose trailing plant covered with tiny star-like, rose-pink flowers, almost hiding the narrow green leaves. It is very well known, very common in gardens and likes a lime-free, leafy soil. Grow it above the

Helichrysum, since it could easily smother it or anything planted in crevices near it. Increase it by cuttings in summer or raise it from seed. The variety '*Rubra compacta*' has deeper pink flowers and is more compact.

Hypericum trailers recommended are *H. reptans* (creeping on ground, crawling); and *H. trichocaulon* (hairy stem). The first trails over rocks and stones on mountain slopes in Sikkim; and in cultivation prospers best on a sunny wall that is reasonably well sheltered in winter. The leaves, evergreen, ovalish and palish in colour, turn yellow or red in late autumn. The open, golden yellow flowers, 2 inches across, are red in the bud and retain some of the colour on the petals during the blooming season, which is from late summer almost till the end of the year. Grow this plant in well-drained, loamy soil that doesn't dry out through the summer months. It is a vigorous trailer that provides a bright patch of yellow on a wall late in the year and doubly valuable on that account.

The other *Hypericum* is a recent introduction. A native of Crete; less vigorous than the other, and a smaller, daintier plant, with small, light green, oblong leaves and reddish-coloured buds which open out into bright yellow flowers during July and August.

Iberis, the perennial Candytuft (*I. sempervirens*), which makes a wide, high mound of hard white flowers, hiding the evergreen leaves, looks too conspicuous growing from a crevice in a tallish wall: it should be put at the top and allowed to trail over. Or it could be grown right at the bottom where it would make a round mass touching the pathway. It looks less out of place on a low rock wall, as mentioned on page 69.

Irises are used by many gardeners for adorning the top of a wall. There are the tall Flags and the dwarfs. Plant the common, practically indestructible, *Iris germanica*, with bright purple, slightly fragrant flowers on high walls and *I. pumila* and *I. chamaeiris*, the Sardinian Iris, which is very like it, on low walls. These three Irises have sword-shaped leaves which come in a tuft and are attractive for most of the year. They all belong to the same class; they are bearded and have produced many charming varieties in shades of yellow, blue, mauve, and there are also cream and pure white ones. All lovely to see growing in rows along the top of a wall in spring. Camillo Luca tells me that the Iris from his native Sardinia needs full sun and well-drained limy soil like the other two, and although completely hardy gives the best show when planted in a cool greenhouse. In the old days there were miniature rockeries in some of the conservatories and the Sardinian Iris was often grown there and vied in colour and beauty with many of the tropical Orchids that bloomed at the same time, *I. chamaeiris var.* 'Moonlight', with pale lemon flowers, is outstanding. (The prefix *chamae-* means: on the ground).

Another conspicuous plant for a wall is the Winter Jasmine, which is perhaps more untidy-looking in such a place than the *Iberis* mentioned above. It is loose and lax and ought really to be planted at the top of a high wall. I grow it myself on a low— 18-inch wall—and it does well there, blooming from November to March. There is nothing to equal it for a show of bright flowers in midwinter. It should be in every garden. The specific name is *Jasminum nudiflorum* (naked-flowered; or perhaps: with hairless-naked flowers). Prune this trailing shrub immediately it has finished blooming—about the end of February. Cut back the shoots which have flowered to promote new strong growths. Never cut into the old wood.

A true dwarf recommended for a wall is *J. Parkeri*, a 6- to 12-inch evergreen shrublet of tufted habit, with pinnate leaves and small yellow flowers in June, usually borne on single stems. A fine plant for the top of a dwarf wall. These Jasmines do best in well-drained loam and are easily propagated by cuttings.

Lewisia (page 28) are more often than not recommended for growing in the alpine house, for apparently they need a more equable climate than ours. But *L. Howellii*, from Oregon (they all come from Western North America) has been found to grow successfully in the vertical crevices of a sunny, sheltered wall facing south. Its small, star-shaped, seven-petalled flowers of a deep rose-pink come on 6-inch stems arising from rosettes of fleshy, narrow, grey-green leaves. It must be grown in deep, rich, lime-free soil in a vertical crevice where the surplus moisture will soon drain away. It blooms in the summer. Protect this choice alpine with a sheet of glass during wet weather and propagate it by seeds.

Lithospermum diffusum 'Heavenly Blue' is the vivid sky-blue evergreen trailer recommended as a companion for the rose-pink trailing *Phlox subulata* 'Vivid' (page 77). Not every gardener chooses it for a wall however and many prefer to grow it in a pocket low down in a rockery, somewhere where the soil is reasonably moist all through the year.

A prolonged spell of dryness will destroy it. Which is strange, many gardeners think, since the plant is a native of the hot dry parts of Southern Europe; common in Spain and the south of France. It is an alpine perhaps that (like many another) doesn't prosper in cultivation; and probably dryness at the roots during our summer droughts and dampness and wet on the hairy stems and foliage during the winter do irreparable damage and finish it off. In time it makes a wide-spreading mass of trailing stems, with small narrowish leaves and deep sky-blue flowers ½ inch across, in terminal spikes. The plant when it succeeds, should be pruned back after flowering. Cuttings of the previous year's shoots should be inserted in equal parts of silver sand and peat under glass to get a supply of new plants. Grow this *Lithospermum* in the same compost, adding if you like a little rubble. If you leave the plant unpruned, it will go on blooming till the autumn.

The following half a dozen plants are recommended by a well-known alpine nurseryman for growing on a retaining wall. Some however really give their best show in the alpine house, others do best in scree soil in the moraine, and yet others are suitable for gardens in warm maritime parts of the U.K.

Such a one is the trailing yellow- or purple-flowered *Mesembry-anthemum edule* (page 72), popularly called the 'Hottentot Fig'. It seldom lives long very far from the sea; in Devon and other warm districts it is naturalized and grows freely on cliffs. It is an expensive plant and best housed near London. A charming colourful trailer for the cold greenhouse.

Omphalodes cappadocica (of Cappadocia) has flowers resembling Forget-me-nots, about ½ inch across in graceful loose clusters and ovalish leaves on long stems; the plant forms clumps with creeping rhizomes and grows well in the crevices of a shady wall. It likes leafy soil with lime rubble in it but not rich soils. Many gardeners find that it is easier to establish in the moraine. It is usually increased by division in spring; or seeds may be sown. It flowers from June to August.

Onosma (page 73) are listed in some catalogues as alpines very suitable for a dry wall but they sometimes succumb to damp and wet as do Androsaces and are therefore often grown in pans in the alpine house. *O. echioides* (*Echium-like*) has flowers like those of *O. tauricum* (the 'Gold Drop'): fragrant, clear yellow and drooping and carried in branched racemes; both foliage (ovalish) and stems are hairy and like protection from our damp winter weather.

Ourisia also like protection from damp and wet and for that reason probably are grown in a sheltered crevice of a dry wall. They also like cool shady places in the summer and are often more of a success in Scotland and the north than in the south. *Ourisia macrophylla* (long or elongated leaves) is not so striking as *O. coccinea* with its scarlet flowers (page 74). The former is a taller plant, with whorls of white flowers about an inch across and bright green, rather downy leaves on long stalks. It blooms in July and should be protected during heavy rains. Propagation is usually by division in the spring. The plant is a native of New Zealand.

Oxalis chrysantha (yellow-flowered) has been grown successfully on walls, in crevices where its creeping stems can run and where it can show off its rosettes of shamrock leaves and charming bright yellow, bell-shaped flowers ($\frac{1}{2}$ inch long) to best advantage. It is a native of Brazil, and blooms in early summer.

Penstemon heterophyllus (having leaves of different shapes) is one of the loveliest of all the race, with its spikes of blue flowers tinged with pink and its greyish-green leaves. The flowers are nearly funnel-shaped; the leaves narrow and pointed. As it is rather tender, a sunny wall is a good place for it; and there, it is best planted low down in a crevice, where its 18-inch slender stems will curve gracefully upward; or it may be planted right at the foot; grow it in ordinary rich garden soil. The variety 'True Blue' is the best form. Keep the soil moist by occasional watering all through the summer. Many gardeners treat these two Penstemons as biennials, sowing the seed under glass in

March. Others take cuttings every autumn and root them in sand in a covered frame. The species is a native of California and in the warm climate there often reaches a height of 5 feet.

Phlox, as already mentioned, are favourite plants for the wall-garden, where they trail down the face in much the same way as the Aubrietias. A charming and well-known association for a wall which gets some shade on it during midday consists of the deep pink *Phlox subulata* 'Vivid' planted on one side of the trailing sky-blue *Lithospermum diffusum* 'Heavenly Blue' and the creeping shrublet *Genista pilosa*, with small yellow pea-like flowers on the other. These shades of pink, blue and yellow blend well and form a charming cascade of colours in May. The important thing to remember when arranging plant associations is to choose those plants that bloom simultaneously. I have tried the richer yellow *Genista delphinensis* instead of *G. pilosa*; but I find that the former blooms a little later than the other two. In fact it is often still in bud when the *Phlox* and the *Lithospermum* are past their best.

Primulas for a dry wall are best grown in the same way as the hardy ferns and the lovely blue *Penstemon heterophyllus* described above. Most of them need a constant supply of moisture at the roots during the growing season and they get it when planted in peaty, leafy soils at the foot of a wall or low down in a crevice. They seldom succeed as wall-top plants. The different kinds of Primroses—the single ones—do well in crevices; so also does *P. marginata*, a charming Primula for the rock-garden, a native of the Maritime and the Cottian Alps (North Italy), a species recommended by alpine nurseries for dry walls. Hillier says: 'A choice plant with white-edged leaves. The soft lavender delicately-scented flowers are large and perfectly formed; March-April. 6 inches. 35p.' The plant described is actually *P. marginata* 'Linda Pope', a hybrid with larger, finer flowers and more toothed, white-edged leaves. Both plants need a well-drained, rich, leafy loam, and should be grown in a sunny crevice with a protruding rock or stone immediately below so that they can send out their rhizomes and woody stems to trail and carry the lovely primrose-like flowers downward. On a flat surface they have a tendency to grow out of the ground. Propagation is simple: by off-sets or by division.

The other Primulas recommended for a dry wall are described under *P.* × *pubescens*; the name covers many delightful hybrids. These plants thrive in sunny crevices, provided the soil retains its moisture through the growing season; it should be leafy or peaty and gritty. All the *Primula* × *pubescens* prosper best in a lower part of a sunny wall. Since they bloom in early spring, they usually get plenty of showery weather to help them on. Like the *P. marginata* Primulas they belong to the Auricula Section (*P. auricula* and *P. rubra* have produced many of these lovely plants). These Primulas are extremely variable; the leaves usually farinose; the flowers, on 3- to 6-inch stems, often some shade of rose-purple, with a white eye.

An enchanting hybrid and one of the oldest in cultivation is *P.* × *pubescens* (downy) *alba* (white). It has roundish tight-packed heads of pure white flowers which are slightly scented and looks lovely running along a low crevice in a sunny wall. I would also like to recommend *P.* × *pubescens* 'Mrs J. H. Wilson', a wonderfully free flowering plant with violet flowers on 4-inch stems, a special favourite of mine and a really good wall Primula. Increase these Primulas by division in spring or early autumn.

Ramonda myconi (of Myconas, a Greek Island) the Pyrenean Primrose and its varieties described on page 29 are not seen in many gardens; I think perhaps because they have the reputation of being very difficult plants to grow and moreover are rather expensive—about 30p a plant. One nursery offers *R. myconi* at this price, the only one; the other two species are rarer in cultivation. They describe it: 'Rosettes of flat, wrinkled leaves; flowers lilac-blue. Should be given a shady, moist site; May. 6 inches.' The rosettes are about 6 inches across, the leaves deeply toothed and with long, reddish hairs; the flowers a charming shade of purple, have conspicuous golden-yellow stamens.

Grow Ramondas in low crevices of a rock wall facing north and give them peaty, leafy soil with a reasonably large admixture of sandy rubble. When well established the rosettes grow into flat clumps with clusters of flowers spreading along the crevices as the plant does in nature; it prospers best in a vertical crevice where surplus moisture cannot collect and rot the crowns and the buds during the winter months. You may, by the way, find your plant shrivelling after a drought, but give it a good soaking and it will soon recover. Propagation is usually by dividing the roots in early spring.

Saponaria ocymoides has already been mentioned as a fine companion for trailing down a sunny wall with the 'Everlasting Flower' *Helichrysum bellidioides*. The Saponaria is a rampant plant, growing 2 or 3 feet in a season, and should be pruned back after flowering. The rarely seen white form *S. ocymoides alba* may be grown with it instead of the *Helichrysum*. Both these Saponarias are best propagated yearly for new stock, for the plants are not always long-lived (see page 107).

Saxifraga of the so-called ENCRUSTED Section (page 84), with their stiff evergreen leaves and sprays of flowers, are charming plants for growing in the crevices of a dry wall. Try the *S. aizoon* Group (page 84); there are dozens of different varieties and they all like well drained, gritty, leafy soils containing lime rubble.

A little known species of the same section is *S. valdensis* (from Mount Baldo in Northern Italy); it is a native of the French Alps and makes a small greyish cushion plant for a sunny crevice, and in early summer produces round heads of small white flowers on 3-inch stems.

For a crevice high up in a shady wall grow *S. lingulata 'Albido'* (tongue-leaved, white-flowered); it has 12-inch stems, with white flowers in arching panicles during early summer. A graceful Saxifrage that needs a high spot to show off its flowers. The leaf rosettes are large and form spreading mats of iron-grey leaves with margins beaded with silver.

There is a tiny 'London Pride' called 'Primuloides, Ingwersen's Var.' which does well in a crevice of a shady wall and is nowhere near as invasive as the type plant. It is only 4 inches high and has bronzy leaves and rich red flowers. For the best results plant it in a crevice a foot or so from the base of the wall and in gritty leafy soil. Water it well when you plant it and continue to do so till it is well established.

Sedums which form mats of fleshy flattish rosettes do well in the crevices of a dry wall. Often their foliage is their chief attraction and is moreover extremely valuable for the patches of colour it provides right through the winter months. These Sedums are best planted low down and left to spread along the crevices and down on to the pathway.

Sedum cauticola (growing on cliffs) is a Japanese species which will trail over the top or from a top crevice; it has glaucous leaves on arching, spreading stems and open flattish heads of rose-purple flowers that bloom in early autumn.

Another Sedum for the top, for a high, dry, hot crevice is *S. pruinatum* (as though frosted over). It has very glaucous foliage and longish slender stems, which carry in late summer yellow flowers in a branched head. The plant is a native of Spain and Portugal.

The two species *S.S rupestre* and *reflexum* are often confounded with *S. pruinatum*. You often get *S. pruinatum* for the *S. rupestre* advertised in catalogues.

S. rupestre (growing on rocks) is a mat-forming Sedum, with glaucous evergreen foliage, which turns red with age (or when the plant is in starved soils), and drooping clusters of clear yellow flowers on stems 8 to 12 inches long. It blooms in July, and always profusely on a sunny wall. This species is native to Western Europe and is found wild in the U.K., mostly on old walls in the West Country. These Sedums are easily propagated by division in early autumn.

S. reflexum (bent back sharply); the flowering shoots, the longest, 12 inches in length, are often reflexed; they carry branched heads of yellow flowers, which are about $\frac{1}{2}$ inch across. A bright-looking trailing Sedum for the top of the wall-garden.

There is a curious form known as *Var. cristatum*, with fasciated stems (abnormally enlarged and flattened), which is occasionally seen growing on the top of a wall. Farrer describes it as a form of *Sedum rupestre* and calls it *Sedum Crista-galli*: 'Only a cockscomb-leaved form ... very monstrous and frightful.' The plant is occasionally offered by nurseries who list it as 'a variety with stems flattened out into a monstrous green cockscomb, often several inches wide. It is an old curiosity of cultivation'.

Grow also *S. spathulifolium purpureum* (page 87) in crevices at the foot of the wall; as birds often attack the fleshy rosettes in winter, pulling them off the face of the wall, presumably in search of insects during the winter, it is advisable to protect the plant with a pane of glass. *Sedum acre* is often grown as a creeping, draping evergreen mat at the top of a wall. And it looks most attractive in winter, with the plum-coloured *S. spathulifolium* below it, at the foot.

Sempervivum are excellent plants for growing in the crevices of a wall, the smaller kinds especially are very decorative there. Like the rosette-forming Sedums mentioned above, they are best set fairly low down on the face so that they can be readily protected with a pane of glass when the birds get busy searching for insects. These thick fleshy plants need more nutriment than the mixture of sand and brickdust recommended for them usually provide; the biggest—those forming large rosettes like *S. grandiflorum* (sometimes 9 inches across)—need loamy soils (page 89), and soils with humus in them; add a little sifted leafmould to the garden loam you use. The 'Cobweb Houseleeks' (page 89) are most picturesque plants for growing along the lower crevices; they are also fine contrasting plants to grow with trailers and creepers that cascade down the face.

The variety *S. arachnoideum glabrescens* (becoming smooth) has rosettes of egg-shaped leaves, and 'cobwebs' that are rather loose and lax; grow it in sandy leafmould in a wall crevice where it will get sun on it all day. The starry, pink flowers come in clusters on 3- to 4-inch stems. There is a charming white-flowered variety found growing in Zermatt, which makes a delightful companion-plant for any of the pink ones. Grow this white variety, if you can get it, in a wall crevice above the others. All the 'Cobweb' Houseleeks prosper in lime-free soils. Push plenty of sifted leafmould and sand into the crevices before you plant them and top-dress them occasionally in this way.

S. arenarium (growing in sand) is among the smallest of the Sempervivums, with light green rosettes about ¾ inch wide (some smaller) and some with their leaves coloured reddish-brown at the tips. The flowers, which are seldom seen in this country, are greenish-white. Grow it in a sunny crevice of light sandy soil. It will make a pretty patch of foliage on a wall for the winter months. It is a species also recommended for growing in troughs and sink-gardens that are so popular with town and city gardeners. Sempervivums flourish quite luxuriantly in the smoky atmosphere of towns and cities.

Tropaeolum are popularly called Nasturtiums. And of these, most people grow the annual bedding or climbing kinds. The climbers can be trained up or down a tallish wall and although they are rather untidy-looking and take up a lot of room, they are reliable flowerers and give a long show of colour practically all through the summer and autumn months. Seeds cost about 5p a packet and may be sown in March (till as late as June) where the plants are to bloom. They flower profusely when grown in poor, sandy soils. In loam or in any fairly rich soil, they produce foliage at the expense of flowers.

The perennial Tropaeolums are quite different and prefer lime-free soils; several need acid sandy leaf soils or peat. They are expensive; and one, *T. polyphyllum*, already mentioned, is a charming creeper to grow along with the blue rock Campanulas (page 103). It is, of course, very beautiful on its own, draping a wall, low or high and its tubers are always planted deep down—about 9 inches—in leafy, gritty soils. The tubers, by the way, are edible, sweetly flavoured, tasting of chestnuts—in Chili, where the plant comes from, they are cooked rather in the way that we cook Jerusalem Artichokes.

The species prized by gardeners for training on walls—house walls usually—is *T. speciosum* (showy), the Scotch Flame Flower, or Flame Nasturtium, which is also a native of Chili; it seems to grow best in a cool moist atmosphere such as that which prevails in Scotland and the North of England. Given a suitable place in cultivation, it will ascend to a height of 15 feet or more. You might wonder where and how it can be grown on a dry wall? I have seen it trained up thin bamboo canes, a young plant left in its pot and sunk in the soil, at the foot of a 4-foot wall.

The soil for this plant is best made up of sifted leafmould and broken sandstone. Most nurseries send out plants established in pots; and they may be sunk in the soil (lime free) close against a wall facing north and trained in the way I have suggested. Shade is essential for this magnificent scarlet creeper (or twiner) and it needs plenty of moisture all through the growing season. It is a fine plant to grow, since its small, scarlet, Nasturtium-like flowers bloom in late summer, and are followed by brownish-red capsules exposing conspicuous seeds the size of peas and of a lovely turquoise-blue colour all through the autumn. You may of course plant it at the top of a fairly high wall and train it down the face, provided little or no sun reaches it.

Yet another perennial species for a wall is the 'Peruvian Nasturtium', *T. tuberosum*; as it is only half-hardy, it should be grown in its pot (sunk in the soil: good deep lime-free leafmould and grit) and lifted and housed from November till late May, when it is safe to put it out again. Its flowers, which bloom in September, are orange and red with long straight spurs; its leaves, five-lobed and long-stalked. A choice climber or trailer for a high sunny wall.

Tunica saxifraga (stone breaker: probably stone dweller) is found growing on sunny rocky banks in the Southern Alps, in the Mediterranean region and as far as Persia. The family is related to *Gypsophila* and many of the flowers are similar in shape and structure to the Dianthus. Our species forms tufts of thin wiry stems, which carry during the summer a succession of small Pink-like flowers, white tinged with rose, and tiny narrow bright green leaves. The plant in full bloom has a charming, light, airy effect and is ideal for an upper crevice of a wall in full sun. Under cultivation this *Tunica* improves and grows larger and moreover, gives a richer colour effect. Grow it in perfectly-drained sandy, leafy soil, and add a little finely-sifted leafmould when you plant it to start it off well. It is a treasure for the wall-garden, not only for its charming appearance but for its long flowering season. There is a double-flowered variety, not so hardy as the type; and *Var. pleniflora*, with white or lilac flowers. These *Tunica* often seed themselves, and they are very prolific and produce plenty of seed. Sow the seed in silver sand and light loam in spring.

Valerian is the popular name of *Valeriana*, of which several alpine species are grown in our rockeries. *V. celtica* is the wonderfully fragrant Nard of the Alps, which is gathered especially for its root, its most fragrant part.

The Red Valerian, which we see on our cliffs and old walls, is not actually a native, but has been naturalized here in the course of centuries. One of its common names, apart from Valerian, is 'Ventnor Pride'; the plant is very common on the cliffs in the south of England and in many parts of the country. And its true name is *Kentranthus (Centranthus) ruber*, which few people use; practically everybody calls it *Valerian*. There are both red and white forms; they grow about 2 feet high and make bushy plants, with attractive pale-green foliage, and flourish in the crevice of walls. The poorer the soil, the finer the flowers. It is one of the easiest of all wall-garden plants: more suitable perhaps (because of its bushy appearance) for fairly high walls. For an immediate effect on a tallish wall, plant seedlings, one above the other in the crevices, leaving about 12 inches between each plant. They will soon spread out and make a fine sheet of colour in summer. Valerian is easily raised from seed sown outside in light sandy soil during March and April. Dobies' keep packets of the red variety; 'Valerian (*Kentranthus ruber*). Useful for borders, dry walls, or for the wild garden. Large heads composed of many rosy-red flowers, 4p.'

Veronica prostrata and *V. whitleyi* are two blue-flowered plants which show their spikes of lovely blue flowers to advantage on a wall. See page 91 for a description of the first. The second is a trailing plant with finely-cut, hairy, light green leaves and clusters of bright blue flowers with white centres; both bloom from June till about August and like a light, loamy soil and a sunny position. Propagate them by division or by cuttings.

Because you haven't a wall-garden, it doesn't follow that you can't grow the plants I have described above. You can grow them all in an ordinary rockery, providing them, if you can, with good flat boulders to creep over or along. Or let them grow in pockets, or in gulleys between two gently sloping parallel rocks.

But to show off their true character, they should be grown draping or trailing over a wall. Which is different from a vertical rock or vertical boulders in a rockery. The wall is a formal structure, obviously built by hand, constructed mostly of horizontally-laid slabs or blocks of stone, and ideally suited for trailing plants. There is room of course for other kinds: for the top, Irises are a perfect choice: appropriately formal-looking plants for growing in rows. And here and there in some of the crevices, one may grow tufted alpines, rosette-plants and a few dwarf shrublets to provide variety and contrast. Colour can best be displayed on a wall; different shades can be better blended and contrasted there than anywhere else in the rock-garden.

CHAPTER 4

The Moraine

What is a moraine? The usual definition is: 'An accumulation of earth and stones carried down and deposited by a glacier.' Further, a 'terminal' or 'end' moraine is a moraine deposited by a glacier at its end when the ice is at its maximum extent and has its own special flora and vegetation nourished by the flow of water percolating through the débris from the ice above and by the vegetable matter brought with it.

And a scree? Most writers speak of it as being the same as a moraine, but this is not the case. A scree is described as a heap of stones or rocky débris, or 'A mass of detritus, forming a precipitous, stony slope upon a mountain-side. Also the material composing such a slope.'

A scree, then, would be easier to make than a moraine with its constant flow of water. Most people, however, use the words 'scree' and 'moraine' interchangeably: scree plants and moraine plants are the same thing; so likewise are scree soil and moraine soil.

Making or building a moraine as part of a small rock-garden isn't a difficult or a lengthy job. Site and position are important. And since many of the plants are tiny and almost stemless, it is best to have it built on a slope, so that the plants can be viewed more easily. At ground level some tiny gem even in full bloom might be missed completely, unless one bent down close to it. The lowest part could be reserved for taller things, or simply strewn with washed pebbles. (You can get special 'Sea-washed pebbles' and 'Essex Grey pebbles' from most masonry firms.)

A moraine in the garden should have some protection from the hot midday sun, which can do a lot of harm to scree alpines during a long dry summer. So let it have a south-west or a west aspect, unless there is some system of irrigation to keep the soil constantly moist, such as a specially perforated water-pipe laid under the soil and connected with the mains. The water can be turned on when it is necessary to give the foundation soil a good soaking. But for a small moraine, which most people want, an ordinary watering-can or a hose with a fine spray may be used during a drought. Give the soil a thorough good soaking with half a dozen cans of rain-water in the spring and it will remain 'wet' all the season.

The system of underground irrigation is not so popular nowadays and constant watering isn't necessary. If the moraine is well constructed, it will absorb water quickly and retain it for a long time. Any system of underground irrigation is therefore unnecessary.

If we take the saucer-shaped dell that we prepare for our rockery (page 21), a miniature moraine could be made on one of the gently sloping sides, leading down to the pathway. It can be curved in shape, like an S, if you like, or not so regular and running or flowing from about a height of 2 feet at the back down to the level ground. The whole length probably will not exceed 4 or 5 feet, and at its widest part, at the bottom, it could be about 3 feet across.

Dig out the soil and support the interior of the small chasm you make (or re-inforce it) with rocks, which will help to hold the scree soil together and in position (prevent it merging with the main body of the soil in the sloping bank) and also help to keep it moist after it has been watered artificially or well soaked with rain.

Crude drainage rocks or stones are put at the bottom—not less than 3 inches in depth—and perhaps a drainage-pipe laid, sloping out in the direction of the pathway, to take away any surplus water that might collect and stagnate after a long spell of wet.

Now you can pause and decide what scree plants you want to grow: some like peaty acid soil; others limy soil (limestone chips or pebbles mixed with chalky loam and leaf soil); yet others limestone chips mixed with pure acid peat; again others seem to prosper in almost pure sand, though their roots are usually long and vigorous and go down deep in search of nutriment in the lower strata. You can, of course, make separate beds or pockets or patches, segregated from one another, for the different kinds of alpines you want to grow. Each will have its own particular type of soil.

Before putting in the scree soil, throw in some broken bricks, preferably small pieces; brick holds moisture for a considerable time. Water this foundation layer thoroughly or leave it exposed to the autumn rains—early autumn is a good time for building. Then put in a layer of old grass turves, soil and roots uppermost, and soak these well.

The final additions are the actual scree-soil, about 9 inches deep, which you can make up yourself or buy from a nursery specializing in alpines; and the topmost layer, at least an inch deep, of stone chippings or pebbles—the half-inch ones are best.

The scree soil, according to the R.H.S. should consist of 75 per cent of grit or medium stone chippings, the balance being equal parts of soil and leafmould. (Partially decomposed leaves, by the way, contain more nutriment than any known garden soil or any of the different sorts of peat you can buy.)

Soak the moraine with rain-water after the inch layer of chippings has been added, and let it settle till as late as the spring, if you like. On the other hand, if you want a spring show, build the moraine at the end of the summer and give it a daily soaking for the best part of a week. You can then set your plants out in late September.

Take the alpines from their pots and plant them carefully, spreading out the roots among the stones, firming them gently and packing plenty of chippings round them. Between the clumps or tufts or spreading mats, and under the latter, I put a few sea-washed pebbles, approximately 2 inches in diameter; or the larger Essex Grey pebbles which are slightly bigger.*

Planting a moraine is exciting work. Don't be tempted to grow too many things however: let in the sun and the rain so that you can see some of the fresh, washed pebbles.

One is usually tempted to make a rush at all the difficult things

* Mentioned on page 121. These pebbles may be used in many parts of the rock-garden. They cost about £15 a ton.

recommended by alpine specialists but later one finds that some would have done better in pots or pans in the alpine house. Things that grow big, like the alpine Rhododendrons, are perhaps more suitable outside than indoors. And at the bottom of the moraine slope, converging on the path, you could plant the Alpine Roses, *Rhododendron hirsutum*, (hirsute: hairy), which will tolerate some lime; and R. *ferrugineum* (rust-coloured, referring to the foliage). Writers list fifty or more Rhododendron species and hybrids suitable for the moraine, more attractive than the two above and there are probably many more. None is cheap. The two mentioned here cost about £1·05 each.

There are dozens of smaller alpines suitable for the average garden-moraine. In the space of a single chapter, it is possible to mention only a very few—the easiest of the most difficult (I hope) and some of the loveliest. All can be obtained from alpine nurseries. Many have been described in Chapter 2; and they will, of course, prosper well in any ordinary rockery, provided they are given the right type of soil and a situation they like.

The *Acantholimon* (page 40) revel in scree conditions. So does *Achillea ageratifolia*, which blooms in July and August; it forms close rosettes of narrow, silvery-white leaves, toothed; and has pure white daisy-like flowers on shortish stems. It makes a delightful companion grown in front of *Allium narcissiflorum*, with nodding, ruby-red flowers, which is described on page 43.

Androsaces like scree conditions and most of them may be grown in the moraine. I add *A. sempervivoides* which my nurseryman advertises as having 'Rosettes of incurved leaves, flowers pink, with a crimson eye; April–May; 2 inches. 25p.' It comes from Northern India: a really striking little plant, carrying tiny heads of Verbena-like pink flowers on short stems, and forming a mat of leaf-rosettes on spreading stolons or runners. Give it a patch of light, leafy, sandy soil, with plenty of chips in it.

Armeria caespitosa (growing in tufts) is a tiny Thrift from the high mountains of Spain, often found at 8,000 feet. A choice little scree alpine with tiny cushions of stiff leaves and round heads of usually rose-lilac flowers in April and May. There are deeper pink garden forms, more striking than the collected plant. 'Beechwood'; deep pink; 'Bevan's Variety'; deep rose.

Asperula suberosa (corky; i.e. the stems) is a very beautiful little plant from Greece; one every alpine gardener wants to grow in the rockery (page 53). It is better in the moraine and best of all in the alpine house. It appreciates a limy scree soil and blooms during June and July.

Campanulas for the ordinary rock-garden are numerous; the choicer ones such as *C. C. zoysii*—always attacked by slugs—and *arvatica* are better in the moraine or even in the alpine house. The first named I cannot buy anywhere at the time of writing; the second is offered by most nurseries and recommended for the scree. Its slender ascending 6-inch stems form tufts, with small heart-shaped leaves and pretty, star-shaped, purple flowers about an inch across, which bloom in July. It is not all that hardy and many people cover it with a cloche through the cold weather. It is found wild in limy screes (in Arvas: *arvatica*) in the Cantabrian Mountains, Northern Spain. Most gardeners propagate it by seed.

Dianthus alpinus, 'the most precious of the race', is an excellent scree Pink and given perfect drainage will thrive either in limy loams or in leafy loams containing lime. There are two very charming varieties, viz. *albus*, with white flowers; and *grandiflora*, with large pink flowers.

D. neglectus, on the other hand, needs a scree pocket of lime-free soil; it has given a fine variety called *Roysii*, which has larger flowers and larger leaves. It must likewise be grown in a lime-free soil.

Edraianthus (see Chapter 2) like lime and a warm sunny place; some gardeners who treasure them as very precious plants grow them in pots in the alpine house. But on the moraine slope, with a protruding, protecting rock behind them, they are safe enough in most of our rock-gardens. *E. pumilo* (rather dwarf) is a cushion-forming Campanula-like plant, with tiny narrow silvery leaves and stemless, funnel-shaped flowers of a rich violet colour, which are at their best in June. A good companion-plant, by the way, for the pink-flowered *Asperula* mentioned above.

E. serpyllifolius, mentioned on page 62, has trailing stems carrying bell-shaped purple flowers in May; they are an attractive deep red in the bud and a striking contrast to the mat or rosette of small green leaves on which they lie. There are two well-known varieties; the largest, finest form is *Var. Major* already described in Chapter 2; *Var. alba* has white flowers. The three plants make a charming trio for a sunny scree slope.

Geranium argenteum (silvery) comes from the mountains of Northern Italy and is listed by several nurseries as 'A choice species with silvery leaves and large clear pink flowers in summer. Scree conditions. 4 inches.' The leaves are finely cut and silky and silvery on both sides, a perfect foil to the dog-rose-like pink flowers. It needs a sunny position and lime in the soil. The purple-flowered variety 'Purpureum' makes a charming background plant for it. The best results are obtained by planting these Geraniums as smallish seedlings. Sow the seed under glass in March and set out the young plants in September.

Lithospermum oleifolium (with leaves like the Olive Tree) is a lime-scree shrubby plant from the Pyrenees. It is apparently rare in nature and not always obtainable at the nurseries. I bought a good specimen some years ago and succeeded in propagating it by cuttings several years running. A local nursery lists it at 50p a plant: 'A rarely seen prostrate shrub, with beautiful azure-blue, bell-shaped flowers; June–September. Needs a sheltered scree or alpine house. 6 inches.' The leaves, narrow-oval, ½ inch long, are grey-green above and silky-white beneath; the flowers are usually a palish blue; but often pink or red tinctures the blue and rather spoils it. A choice shrubby spreading plant for the bottom part of the moraine garden, especially for a spot where lime is likely to seep through from the higher part of the slope. It is not such a striking plant, I think, as the 'Heavenly Blue' *Lithospermum*, which we grow in the crevices of a dry-wall (page 110).

Myosotis, the alpine Forget-me-nots, are difficult outside the scree or the alpine house. Most nurseries advertise three or four different kinds. The favourite one seems to be *M. rupicola* (growing in rocky places), the one Reginald Farrer calls the Queen of all the alpine Forget-me-nots. 'In the garden ... it delights especially in the moraine.' It is a small, dense plant, forming tight cushions about 2 inches high, which, from May to August, are covered with large azure-blue flowers. Grow it in a limy pocket or patch at the top of the scree slope.

Petrocoptis lagascae is an uncommon rock-plant from the

Pyrenees that more often than not succumbs to our winter wet
and is therefore nearly always raised annually from seed (which
it produces in great abundance). It is listed however as a perennial
alpine, a tufted plant, with glaucous, leathery narrow leaves and
big (¾-inch) rose-carmine flowers, with a white centre. They are
produced very freely from May to August. In many catalogues it
appears under the name of *Lychnis Lagascae*—described by a local
nursery as 'an old and deservedly popular alpine plant from Spain
and the Pyrenees, covered in late summer with numerous bright
rose-pink flowers, each ½ inch wide. The plant is 3–4 inches high,
and needs a rich, light soil drained to perfection. Best in the
moraine. Valuable for its late blooming habit. Well-rooted specimens in pots, 20p each.'

Farrer, however, doesn't think very highly of it and puts the
species *P. pyrenaica* and its variety *grandiflora rosea* first. Both have
larger flowers of a pure pale pink. But neither unfortunately is
listed in any of the catalogues I have at hand.

Potentilla nitida (smooth and lustrous) is a gem for the limestone
scree, but not easy under cultivation, refusing to bloom freely or
often not at all. And this happens when it is given well-nigh
perfect growing conditions, viz. full sun on a moraine slope and
soil consisting of deep limestone scree over a bed of sandy loam.
The plant, a native of the Alps of Southern Europe, is about 3
inches tall, with silky-silvery leaves, palmate or lobed—the shape
of the palm of the hand—and wild-rose-like flowers an inch
across, often a good clear pink but sometimes a deep rose-pink
and occasionally white. It is a tufted plant eventually forming a
mat of attractive foliage and flowers, the latter unfortunately
sparse at all times. The flowering season is from June to late
August. The plant is propagated by cuttings or by division of the
roots.

Primulas which are listed in catalogues as difficult are usually
best grown in pots or pans and housed under glass as already
mentioned (page 80). Two quite rare species from the mountain
ranges of South-West China are recommended for the moraine.
One is *Primula nutans*, page 80 (nodding, drooping), which has
close clusters of drooping violet-blue flowers—funnel-shaped
and fragrant—borne at the end of 12-inch stems, which are lightly

powdered, and rise from rosettes of soft hairy polyanthus-like leaves. It blooms in early June. The plant often blooms but once then dies; but if it grows well and prospers, it sets plenty of seed. Sow the seed in September. You often see this primula in the alpine house; but it should be tried first in the moraine.

The other species is *P. Viali* which, carrying its flowers in spikes like a tiny miniature Red-hot Poker (*Kniphofia*), is most unlike any other Primula we grow. The leaves, long and ovalish, do however resemble the leaves of many of the Asiatic Primulas. The foliage is genuinely Primula-foliage. The spikes are composed of small lavender-blue flowers with scarlet unopened buds at the tips. The plant blooms in June and July.

Both these species need perfectly-drained soil, containing plenty of light leafy soil or peat and limestone chips. And they need a semi-shady position.

P. takedana, a native of Japan, is very rare and expensive (50p a plant) and best suited to a patch of peaty, gritty soil on a scree slope. In its natural habitat it is found in moist crevices of high rocky mountain slopes, and in cultivation needs perfectly-drained situations during the wet winter months. The leaves are roundish, deeply toothed and hairy, and the thin, hairy scapes rise up 3 to 5 inches, carrying loose clusters of white flowers. It blooms in May and is easily raised from seed.

Pulsatilla vernalis (vernal, appearing in the spring) is one of those alpines that grow high up on snow-covered mountains—our plant comes from the European Alps; and it is more often than not (like many high alpines) a little difficult. It is sometimes grown in the alpine house but should always be given a trial first in the moraine. I find that it does very well there. Our species, one of the Pasque Flowers or Easter Anemones (the genus *Pulsatilla* is closely related to *Anemone*), is described by a local nursery as 'A choice and very beautiful alpine. Given the Award of Merit in 1950. 4 inches tall. 30p.' In the lower valleys, and in our gardens, it grows taller. The flowers, erect and somewhat goblet-shaped, are white, tinged outside with violet-lavender, and covered with silky, brown hairs; the leaves, hairy and coarsely cut, form an open rosette close to the soil and help to protect the buds during the winter weather. Propagation is usually by

Anemone nemorosa, the Wood Anemone: grow it in the Alpine Lawn.

Muscari, the Grape Hyacinth, an early spring bulb for the rock garden.

Crocuses blooming next to a Sedum in mid-winter.

Androsace sarmentosa var Chumbyi, one of the easiest of the Androsaces. It needs a sunny place.

Sedum spathulifolium purpureum will grow practically anywhere in the rockery. Attractive all through the year, with its fleshy plum coloured foliage.

An Alpine Geranium, with dog-rose-like flowers. Lovely in a limy, sunny
moraine.

seed. This species likes an open sunny place in the moraine, and a rich, peaty scree soil preferably without lime in it.

Ranunculus parnassifolius (with leaves like those of Parnassus, that is, oval or heart-shaped and dark green); this plant was first mentioned in the Introduction (page 10): the lovely white alpine Buttercup, a difficult plant to grow in the rock-garden. Not many nurseries stock it. It is propagated by division of the roots or by sowing the seeds as soon as they are ripe, usually in late summer. Some collectors say it is an easy plant—Farrer does—provided, according to him, it is grown in damp places 'of the finest silt' (which is a sediment deposited by water). It likes a sunny spot in rich, leafy soil containing plenty of limestone chippings.

In nature it is found in the highest limestone screes of the Pyrenees and the Alps of Eastern Europe; and in midsummer it blooms, bearing its big white Buttercup-like flowers in clusters on 3-inch stems, which arise from the radical leaves, dark green and slightly woolly and margined with red. It is at its best in these high screes, the flowers are bigger, and the pink flush on the outsides of the petals more conspicuous. On lower slopes, in warmer parts of Southern Europe, the flowers are usually smaller and not so striking. It is best to see this plant in bloom first at a nursery before buying it. Inferior kinds are sometimes offered.

Saxifraga on the whole like stony places and rocky slopes and practically all the *Kabschia* and *Engleria* Section do best in the scree. *S.* × *apiculata* is described on page 85, and the *Burseriana* group in the next chapter, which deals with the alpine house and some of the more intractable alpines that are grown there.

The hybrid 'Riverslea', of the Kabschia-Engleria Section, is a plant about 2 inches high forming a mat of silver-grey rosettes, spangled in spring with tiny purplish-rose flowers with deeper crimson centres. It needs a leafy, gritty scree soil that retains its moisture all through the growing season. (It has been grown successfully—out of the scree—in tufa rock.) Propagation is by stem cuttings and by separating the small single rosettes and rooting them in sand under glass.

All the Saxifrages belonging to the Kabschia–Engleria Section are usually propagated in this way. And they flourish in lime-stone-scree soil, with plenty of chippings round them. There are many of them; most alpine nurseries list about a couple of dozen. I recommend the following. *S. ferdinandi-coburgi*, a native of the Rhodope Mountains in Bulgaria, blooms in spring; the flowers, red in the bud, are golden-yellow and are carried on 3-inch stems that arise from silvery-grey rosettes. A bright, lovely plant for the cold English spring. *S. juniperifolia*, the juniper-scented Saxifrage: not so striking in flower as most of the Kabschias, but forms attractive sharply pointed cushions of dark green foliage; the flowers are tiny, yellow and come in small clusters during the summer. *S. marginata* is a finer plant, with sprays (2–3 inches) of large, white flowers, which spring up from rosettes of fleshy, green leaves margined with silvery-white. *S. stribrnyi*, another species from the Rhodope Mountains, has silver margined leaves and crimson-purplish flowers on 6-inch stems; it blooms in early summer; a fine Engleria Saxifrage. These Saxifrages cost about 25p each and are supplied well rooted in pots for immediate planting out.

S. oppositifolia (opposite-leaved) forms trailing mats of interlacing stems with small dark green, usually rounded, leaves and rose-purple terminal flowers on inch stems; they are cup shaped as a rule, ¾ inch across and come in profusion during March and April. There are some well-known varieties, all attractive plants for the limestone scree; nurseries usually offer half a dozen or so. The most reliable, the one that seems to live longer than the others is *Var. Splendens* with largish deep rose, stemless flowers. *Var. latina* has also largish flowers, pink in colour, and its leaves are tipped with silver; a more upright plant than the others— about 2 inches tall. The white flowered form is *Var. alba*. There are some good and some very inferior plants offered under this name. The R.H.S. describes *alba* as having 'flowers, poor, white, starry . . .' Hillier lists: '*Var. Alba*: starry white flowers. 1 inch. Award of Merit 1963.' Obviously a good form. From the same list: '*Var. Coccinea*. Crimson flowers. A.M. 1906. 1 inch.' *S. oppositifolia* is found wild in Europe and in Northern Asia and North America—some fine specimens are found on rocky heights in our northern counties, and some at sea-level in Scotland; they flourish on both limestone and granite rocks; in the garden the varieties mentioned here do best in a position sheltered from the hot midday sun, in limestone scree that is always moist.

Silene acaulis (without an evident stem) is known as the Moss Campion and the Cushion Pink (see also page 89). It has a wide distribution in the Northern Hemisphere and is occasionally found in the U.K. All collectors recommend it for the moraine, since it blooms more freely there in deep scree limestone soil than in the ordinary rockery where often after a longish period the soil is apt to dry out. The plant makes dense tufts of bright green foliage, the leaves are narrow, grass-like and about ½ inch long; the flowers carried on single very short stems, are star-shaped, rose-pink and about ½ inch wide. The plant is in bloom from June till late August as a rule. If you can, set it in front of a clump of *Gentiana verna*, a dwarfer plant with vivid blue star flowers (see page 140). Both revel in limestone scree and they make a delightful association for the moraine.

Last on our list is the rarely seen *Thlaspi rotundifolium* (with round leaves), a native of the Alps, a plant which in cultivation should be grown in moist limestone-scree soil. It is a tufted plant, with ovalish or nearly circular, grey-green leaves and small Iberis-like rose-lavender flowers that are very fragrant, especially in the wild. Farrer became poetical about the plant and wrote paeans to its beauty and fragrance.* In the rock-garden, even in the moraine, it often isn't long-lived and is therefore nearly always raised annually from seed, or propagated by cuttings taken during April and May. As there are so few alpines with such richly fragrant flowers, it is well worth growing several plants together in a good-sized pan under glass. Many specialists say it gives a better show in the alpine house.

* In his book *The English Rock-Garden*: 'All the slopes are set with those fragrant rosy tuffets, concise and ample and free, cushions of lilac sweetness . . .'

CHAPTER 5

Alpines Under Glass

It is not only rare, difficult plants that we grow in the alpine house, but the precocious flowerers like miniature Daffodils, winter Crocuses, Anemones and Cyclamen. They have tough little bulbs or tubers that withstand the hard frosts, but their flowers quickly freeze and are soon spoiled. Under glass—alpine house, cold greenhouse, or frame—the plants are safe: the flowers don't freeze and they are safe too from slugs and birds. Many choice Campanulas—*C. Zoysii* particularly—are soon devoured by slugs. The R.H.S. says of this species: 'Plenty of chips and rubble, and sufficient moisture, and above all, and above every other Campanula, protection from slugs.' The only place for it is the alpine house, the only place likewise for many other plants (our last mentioned: *Thlaspi rotundifolia*, which slugs like, is often grown there).

Alpines which grow in the mountains high above the clouds are dormant till the deep snows melt, then they bloom safely in a dry, warm sunny atmosphere. But in the lowlands (in cultivation) below cloud level and shrouded in fog and mists for the best part of the winter, they sprout prematurely and come into bloom in the relatively warm air. Then comes a hard frost which destroys the open or partly open flowers. A heavy fall of snow in March followed by a few hours' brilliant sunshine can destroy a magnificent show of alpine blossom. Indoors we may be limited to a single pot or a pan but at least the flowers are safe and delight us till they fade naturally and die. In the garden there is usually too much humidity and too much frost deep down in the soil for many high alpines to prosper well. Humidity can be controlled more or less in the alpine house and deep hard frost in the soil excluded. Much can be done for certain rare alpines in the moraine;

much more indoors, especially during the winter and early spring months.

After they have finished flowering, most of the plants must be stood outside in the air in a cold frame or a plunge bed (made up of sifted ashes and pebbles) and left till about October, when they are brought indoors again. There is no question of forcing, of course: the alpine house must be kept cold.

Much has been written about the ideal alpine house, about its size and construction. But an ordinary cold greenhouse can be used for all the alpines the average gardener wants to grow. It's not necessary to build a house specially, unless you have a very large collection of plants.

A glass lean-to built on to the sunny side of the house is much less suitable than the ordinary cold greenhouse, for it gets too hot. And usually the only way of ventilating it is by leaving the door open. A lean-to with a northern or a north-eastern aspect is better; but the most suitable places are those that stand away from the house. They should run preferably from south to north or from south-west to north-east, so that they get all the sun possible. The usual span-roofed structure (the arch principle: the inverted V-shape) built on a brick base is the type recommended. The height from the floor to the ridge (the uppermost part where the two sloping sides meet) is usually about 9 feet; the width about 14 feet; the length is usually decided upon by the owner, if he is having the alpine house built. It is possible now however to buy the house in sections and to assemble these oneself.

For the light airy conditions and low humidity necessary for the healthy growth of the plants, free ventilation is essential and is provided by top and side windows. During a long hot summer spell it may be necessary to leave these open the whole time. Heating should only be necessary to dry the atmosphere on exceptionally damp foggy days. The modern paraffin heater and the electric fan heater, which provides continuous forced air heating (when it is required), are both efficient and popular nowadays; they can be turned on or switched on when necessary and will prevent condensation on the glass and the consequent danger of drip.

At all times the glass must be kept clean; and it must also be shaded during periods of hot sunny weather, otherwise the plants in full bloom begin to fade before they should; light muslin blinds fixed along the roof are the best and are easily drawn.

Water-tanks should be kept outside; use rain-water whenever you can. When there is a shortage, fill the tanks and let the water stand for a day or so; add Sequestrene for lime-hating plants such as Rhododendrons and others I have mentioned in the text.

The alpine frame—much less popular than a glasshouse—presents no watering problems, however: you simply leave the 'light' off (the framed glazed cover) and let the rain in. During the winter months, of course, it may be necessary to keep the frame covered for long periods, only lifting the 'light' occasionally on to supports for the purpose of ventilation.

The plants themselves may be set out directly into suitable soils or planted in pots or pans and plunged into sifted ashes and sand.

Soil: It should slope a little in the frame from the top to the bottom. The acid, lime-free portion must occupy the top section; that containing lime the bottom. In this way no lime by percolation can reach those plants that dislike it.

Containers: Pans not very deep are best used for surface-rooting plants such as Rhododendrons and Azaleas; pots for deeper rooting things; and those called Long Toms or Clematis Pots are exceptionally deep and necessary for plants that make long tap-roots.

Adonis amurensis is mentioned by the R.H.S. as 'A good plant for alpine house; several varieties occur in Japan.' *A. amurensis* 'Flore Pleno' (with double flowers), grows well in a deep pot of equal parts of sandy loam and sifted leafmould and blooms under glass as early as January. Its flowers have a touch of green in them and are perhaps not quite so attractive as the single variety described on page 42; this plant has purer yellow flowers with a boss (or bunch) of golden-yellow stamens. There are white, pink and rose forms, but these are not commonly offered by nurseries.

Androsaces, according to one rock-garden enthusiast, should all be grown under glass. I have mentioned several that do well in the rockery and the moraine, and *A. lanuginosa*, a choice hairy, silky trailer for the wall-garden. I have seen them all in pots and pans in the alpine house, the trailer in a tall Long Tom and ready for re-potting. *A. alpina* (page 45) does well in a pot of lime-free, leafy, gritty soil; woodlice seem to make for this plant. (These pests sometimes invade glasshouses and must be trapped and destroyed—use hollowed out pieces of apple or potato.) It must be mentioned here that not only woodlice, but greenfly, scale, and even slugs will be found in some glasshouses—and frames— chiefly where there is dirt, rotting wood (perhaps a shelf) and bad or inadequate ventilation.

A. helvetica (of Switzerland) is a high alpine found also in Austria, with hairy, silky rosettes, from which grow single white flowers about ¼ inch across. In a good healthy specimen they grow in profusion and cover the whole plant during May—late April in the alpine house. A cultural hint concerning watering: do not wet the foliage: use a watering-can with a narrow tapered spout which carries the water directly to the soil in the pot without touching the leaves. (Hairy, woolly leaves are best unwetted.)

Through the winter months this species must have a dry resting period. It shouldn't be necessary to use any heat, but the atmosphere must be kept very dry. A good-sized pot or pan will enable the plant to spread. It must be perfectly drained and contain a good deep mixture of loose loamy soil with plenty of limestone chippings. Propagate it in August by offsets grown on in moist cool sand and leafsoil.

A. imbricata has been tried in the rockery, given a sheltered sunny spot there, with an overhanging rock to keep off the winter wet, but hasn't lived very long (see page 13). As its hairy leaves readily absorb moisture, which often causes them to damp off, it is more satisfactory in a glasshouse. The leaves are very white and downy, small and overlapping (imbricate: like scales or roof-tiles), forming smallish rosettes; the flowers whitish or pink are about ¼ inch across and bloom in early summer. Its natural habitat is the granite precipices of the Alps; in cultivation it does best under glass in pans or pots of lime-free leafy gritty soil. This species is not so attractive, I think, as *A. villosa* (shaggy, or with long white hairs), a plant 2 or 3 inches high, with small, hairy rosettes, forming a dense mat, from which arise white or pink flowers with a carmine eye. The variety 'Grandiflora', with larger finer flowers, is more striking. All these Androsaces need a dry atmosphere during the winter months. After their flowers have faded, about July, they should be stood outside in an open frame, or plunged in a bed of ashes. The sun and the warm air benefit them enormously. These Androsaces may also be tried in the moraine.

Anemones that bloom in winter are often grown in the alpine house; they can be enjoyed there or brought into the living-room to provide a show of colour for a few weeks. On the whole Anemones in pots last longer in bloom than those that are cut for decoration. These early flowerers are much appreciated and usually ahead of those grown outside. The two blue-flowered species, *A. apennina* and *A. blanda* (page 47), both about 6 inches tall, do well in pots of deep, sandy loam. The first (from the Apennines, Italy), with divided leaves rather like those of our common Wood Anemone, needs protection from the sun and blooms a little later than the other, which is often in full flower in January. Sink both plants in their pots in a shady place outside after they have finished blooming and bring them indoors again about October.

Other winter-blooming bulbs (tubers and corms), particularly those mentioned at the beginning of the chapter, should be dealt with in the same way. Cyclamen need shading from the sun. There are some fine specimens of *Cyclamen pseudibericum*, with deep carmine flowers, to be seen in the alpine house at Wisley (the R.H.S. Gardens).

Aphyllanthes monspeliensis (from Montpelier, South of France) is noted for its charming deep blue star-shaped flowers; a liliaceous plant, with slender rush-like stems (4 inches tall) bearing at the tips the flowers above clusters of grass-like chaffy bracts. It needs a pan of sandy, gritty peat and in that mixture will thrive in the moraine or even the rockery, with overhead winter protection. But it is a favourite alpine house plant, and blooms in early summer. Since it resents root disturbance, it is usually increased by seed. After some years in the same pot, however, root division might be a good thing.

Arabis blepharophylla (with fringed leaves) is tender (page 51); according to the R.H.S. Dictionary: 'apt to be killed in hard winters . . .' It is a native of California, about 4 inches tall, and bears its large Arabis rose-purple flowers in early March under glass. The soft green leaves are the usual Arabis type. Give it a pot of well-drained, leafy sandy soil containing rubble or chippings. Propagate this Arabis by cuttings—3 inches long inserted in moist sandy soil, in the glasshouse—or by division in September.

Armeria caespitosa is the Spanish alpine Thrift recommended for the moraine (Chapter 4); it and its varieties are delightful little plants too for the alpine house, blooming there some weeks earlier (April) than they do outside.

Asperula suberosa, like the Armeria, does well in the moraine, with a pane of glass over it during the winter; but most gardeners prefer to grow it in a pot under glass; for its grey silver woolly foliage suffers badly in wet weather, which often causes it to damp off. It seldom lives for very long in the ordinary rock-garden (see Chapter 2). *Bellis rotundifolia caerulescens*, the Blue Daisy, mentioned in the same chapter, is another good plant for a pot.

Campanula for the rock-garden are on the whole hardy plants and give a good show of massed mauvish-blue or white flowers in a pocket, or trailing down a wall. Some, however, are attacked and destroyed by slugs: *C. Zoysii* (pages 57 and 125) is never safe in the garden. And *C. isophylla* (having equal leaves) is a semi-trailing bellflower with open lilac-blue flowers and ovalish, toothed pale green leaves, and only successful in warm sunny sheltered gardens in the far south. In Britain it is best grown in a pot of loose, leafy, gritty soil in the dry atmosphere of the alpine house. Other bellflowers that are safer under glass are *C. alpina*, dark blue bells (the plant sometimes flowers itself to death); *C. cenisia*, bright clear blue, funnel-shaped bells; *C. elatines*, blue-purple. Slugs go for all of them. They should be propagated by division or by taking young cuttings in spring.

Daphne petrae (growing in rocky or stony ground) is found in crevices of sheer precipices in mountainous country around Lake Garda, Northern Italy. This is a tiny, spreading evergreen shrub (about 6 inches high), which in May is covered with clusters of tubular-shaped rose-pink, very fragrant flowers, hiding completely the small narrowish leaves. Although it is perfectly hardy, it is mostly grown in pots in an alpine house, the reason being probably that it can be more easily and better tended there, especially as regards keeping it constantly supplied with water. The soil must be light, peaty or leafy and full of coarse grit. The variety *grandiflora*, is a rather bigger plant with larger flowers. Both plants have been grown successfully at the top of a sunny scree slope by artfully sinking them in their pots deep in the limestone chips. *D. petrae* needs plenty of sun wherever it grows —under glass it must not be scorched up, of course. Propagation is by layering, cuttings, or by grafting.

Draba dedeana resembles the common species described in Chapter 2. Our species is a small cushion-shaped plant with bright green tiny leaves in dense rosettes and white flowers in small clusters on 3-inch stems. The variety *Zapeteri* has loose clusters of snow-white flowers. Both are natives of Spain and both have been grown successfully in crevices in rockeries and wall-gardens. But as they suffer badly from excessive wet during the long winter, they are mostly grown in the alpine house. Light, leafy, gritty soil and a sunny place are necessary. Do not water these Drabas overhead but stand the pots in receptacles containing a little rain water till the soil is well-saturated. Propagation is usually by careful division of the plants and by rooting the pieces or rosettes.

Edraianthus (sometimes listed as *Wahlenbergia*) have been grown successfully in the rockery, the moraine and the alpine house. They do better in warm sunny gardens in the south than they do in the midlands and the north; in these parts they are best grown in pots and pans. Put plenty of drainage material at the bottom and fill up with a light, gritty loam.

Ferns are probably grown in pots as much as they are in the garden. And there is a great variety of dwarf kinds not above 9 inches tall that prosper well in an alpine house which can provide plenty of shade and fresh air for them. In fact their foliage, often delicately formed and fragile, is better under glass than out in the garden: rain and blustering winds frequently ruin many beautiful ferns. Of prime importance in their cultivation are shade and moisture. Both conditions are easily provided under glass: keep the blinds drawn during sunny spells—or move the plants to a shady spot in the glasshouse—and stand the pots in receptacles containing a little water.

There are no finer foil plants for growing along with flowering alpines, especially the more exotic kinds such as *Lewisias: Lewisia brachycalyx* is strongly recommended for the alpine house.

And to accompany it, say, in a pot behind it, try the Maidenhair Fern *Adiantum pedatum* (like a bird's foot, or finely divided); it is hardy—outside it would need a shady sheltered spot, perhaps at the bottom of the wall-garden, and should be planted in a mixture of equal parts of leafmould, loam and coarse sand. Under glass, where it is always a great success, it often reaches a height of 2 feet; from the thin, wiry-looking black stems, branch out graceful finely-divided bright green fronds. A delightful background plant to practically any of the taller-growing alpines. This species is found wild in the Himalaya, China, Japan and North America. Keep the soil moist all through the growing season. A dwarfer species, and a native one, is *A. Capilus-Veneris*, the hardy Maidenhair Fern, found growing in the crevices of caves near our warm sea-coasts. The stems are not taller than 9 inches; they are black and carry finely divided deep green segments. It refuses to live for long in the garden; and is almost invariably grown in a smallish pot; it needs equal parts of fibrous peat, leafmould and limestone rubble. Set the rhizomes on top of the soil, and have plenty of coarse drainage material at the bottom of the pot. A lovely airy foliage plant to stand behind the deep blue-flowered *Aphyllanthes* (mentioned above), with its rush-like stems.

Several hardy ferns have been described that were suitable for growing in the crevices of a shady wall. *Asplenium adiantum-nigrum*, 'Black Spleenwort' or the 'Black Maidenhair' as it is sometimes called, with its dark green delicate foliage, is one; it was recommended for growing with the Pyrenean Primrose (*Ramonda myconi*), which likes a moist crevice in a north wall. Both plants do well, and look beautiful together, in pots in a shady part of an alpine house. You might try them together too in some sort of decorative container, or a sink or a trough, which is often used for growing the tiniest alpines in to make a miniature garden for a town garden or perhaps for a window-sill.

There are plenty of other dwarf kinds. The following are excellent for pots or pans or for growing in a sink-garden.

Adiantum venustum, with graceful pale green fronds; 6 inches; *Asplenium trichomanes*, with thread-like, black stems (3 to 6 inches tall) and tiny green lobes; *Cryptogramma crispa*, the 'Parsley Fern', with finely-divided, bright green fronds; 4 inches. (On the whole ferns are rather more expensive than alpines.)

This little fern is a charming background plant for *Gentiana verna*, which is described as the most difficult of all the Gentians to grow; it is mentioned in Chapter 2; recommended there as a good alpine for a pot. The diverse forms are not as a rule offered by nurseries; and anyhow perhaps nobody wants a white *G. verna*, or a pale blue one or the purple ones from the Dolomites. The finest specimens to grow are said to come from mountainous regions in western Ireland. The flowers are often $\frac{1}{2}$ inch wide and an inch tall, with their five petals spreading outward in a flat star shape; and the colour is the deepest glowing blue to be found in the floral world. In a pot or a pan or in the sink-garden, plant it in a mixture of 1 part sifted leafmould to 2 parts of coarse sand, and put a deep layer of sharp drainage material at the bottom of the pot.

Helichrysum, the 'Everlasting Flowers', are often grown in pots under glass to protect them from our winter damp and wet. Even the toughest, *H. bellidioides*, recommended for the wall-garden, is best when protected during the winter months by a pane of glass. Certainly *H. selago* does better in the alpine house than outside. It is often described as a Cupressus-like shrublet (about 12 inches high), with tiny leaves, $\frac{1}{8}$ inch long (white and woolly underneath), pressed close against the wiry interlacing stems; the flowers are white and small and borne on single stems. A local alpine nursery lists it as 'A shrublet from New Zealand for the sheltered scree or the alpine house, where its silver-green woolly foliage is safe from excessive wet. White everlasting flowers in summer; 65p.' It is best raised from cuttings, struck under glass in late summer.

H. frigidum (cold, frosty: perhaps because of its white, downy appearance) is a dwarfer shrublet; a native of Corsica, where it's very warm, and where the plant grows in high rocky places. It is clothed with silky, white down, and the flowers, pure white and papery, are about ½ inch across, and live a long time. This species is scarce and difficult to get at the moment. It should be increased by cuttings, like the other. Both need light, loamy soil containing leafmould and plenty of grit.

Jeffersonia dubia is a shade-loving, Anemone-like plant from the forests of Manchuria, where it grows in cool leafy soil and flowers before its leaves are fully developed. (It looks rare and tender.) The leaves are roundish and lobed with an attractive violet tinge to them and come on 3-inch stems: the flowers (Anemone-like) are about 1¼ inches across and exquisitely coloured lavender-blue; they bloom in May and June. Like the ferns described above, it needs a shady place in the alpine house; the soil should be lime-free, rich: composed of equal parts of sifted leafmould and coarse grit. It is usually increased by careful division of the roots.

Lewisia Howellii was recommended for a warm dry crevice in the wall-garden; more often, however this plant and the other few species obtainable are grown in pots under glass, where they are safe from damp and wet. It is a beautiful alpine for a pot.

L. tweedyi has been called the most sensational beauty of all the family. It forms rosettes or tufts of fleshy, spoon-shaped leaves, from which spring up short stems carrying the large waxen flowers—two or three together—of a soft apricot or a palish pink colour. The loveliest by far of the evergreen section. Throughout the growing and flowering season it likes an ample supply of water, but drier conditions during the resting period. Which conditions are necessary of course for most plants grown in pots and pans under glass. *L. L. brachycalyx* and *rediviva* have been grown successfully in rockeries and moraines but they give a better show and seem longer-lived indoors. The first, with solitary white satiny flowers 1½ inches wide on 1-inch stems, has fleshy leaves; the plant dies down completely after flowering. *L. rediviva* (renewed) is the 'Bitter Root'; the fleshy, edible roots of which are much enjoyed by the Indians of North America. The leaves, narrow, longish and fleshy, come in rosettes and die away at the time of the plant's flowering (in May, usually, under

141

glass); the flowers open out at the end of 1-inch stems and look like miniature water-lilies—white, sometimes pale pink. A delightful pot plant. Lewisias like well-drained, light, leafy soils containing coarse grit and they are increased by division or by seeds.

Nerines are considered by most gardeners to be suitable only for the alpine house or the cold greenhouse (page 26). *N. sarniensis* (of Guernsey) is the popular one; the bulbs were said to have been washed ashore from a wrecked ship off the island and to have been first grown in gardens near the sea. Nerines like perfectly-drained soil composed of fibrous loam or peaty soil with some coarse sand, *and* to be left alone to get really potbound. Leave the bulbs in the same pots for years. The clusters of salmon-pink flowers (of *N. sarniensis*) come on stems 2 feet or more long. They bloom in autumn, the bulbs needing then plenty of moisture; the narrow, green leaves develop after the flowers. Keep the plants very dry all through the summer resting period. There are several good varieties: 'Miss E. Carter' is famous for its remarkable flowers—deep red, large and numerous.

Onosma albo-roseum (*albo-pilosum*) is close to the 'Gold Drop' plant we grow in the rock-garden (page 74). Stems and leaves are grey with silvery down (often spoiled in the wet); the flowers, tubular, come in arching sprays on 6-inch stems and are first white then turn deep rose-pink. This Onosma is seldom a success in our gardens. It requires the same soil and the same treatment as the other species.

× *Phyllothamnus erectus* is an evergreen hybrid heath-like shrub between *Phyllodoce empetriformis* and *Rhodothamnus chamaecistus*. It is seldom more than 8 inches high, and is of spreading habit, with downy branches and tiny leaves ½ inch long; the flowers come in clusters during early summer and are roughly saucer-shaped, ½ inch across, rose-purple, on slender stems. It needs a lime-free, leafy soil, perfect drainage in its pot and partial shade. Propagation is by cuttings. It is not a long-lived plant and often begins to decline after about six years. In full bloom it is an excellent companion for the glowing, intense blue *Gentiana verna*—also not very long-lived—both are often grown together in the trough- or sink-garden. In a flattish wide pan they could be planted together, the Gentian in front of the shrub. In full bloom, the two in a pot stood in a bowl would make a charming centre-piece for a table decoration.

Phyteuma comosum (growing in tufts or bearing a tuft) is hardy enough, but like many low-growing alpines is often attacked and devoured by slugs. It is best in a pot in the alpine house. Collectors speak of its flourishing luxuriantly in tiny crevices on the perpendicular face of hard limestone rocks and cliffs—where probably slugs can't reach it—and making an attractive show of small blue inflated, flask-like flowers in clusters among ovalish, sharp-toothed (rather Holly-like) leaves. Difficult to reach, they say. *P. comosum*, from Austria and Northern Italy, is of tufted habit, about 3 inches tall and bears its curiously-shaped flowers in July. It is easily propagated by division. Spring is the right time. Grow the plant in a light, loamy soil containing plenty of lime rubble. I have seen it growing (but not really flourishing) in a cavity made in soft tufa rock.

Primulas are a varied race of plants. There are kinds suitable for the ordinary rockery (usually planted in shady crevices); the wall-garden; the moraine; the woodland and the water-garden (often grown *in* water), and in pots under glass. The last named are the difficult species as stated in Chapter 2, page 80 ('*Primula forrestii* which too often succumbs to winter wet . . .'); and also the tender species that must be wintered under glass. *P. allionii* (page 80) and *P. forrestii,** for instance, can be better fostered and tended in pots in the alpine house—shaded, watered, fed, etc. The tender species are always grown in pots or pans. They are useful plants of remarkable beauty for decorating the alpine house during the autumn, winter and early spring months. In summer they are put outside in the frame, into plunge beds (sifted ashes and rubble). They are popularly known as Chinese Primulas and are easily raised from seed. Dobies' have a good variety of these Primulas, small packets costing round about 8p. The chief types are *P. malacoides, P. obconica,* and *P. sinensis*—the newest brightly-coloured horticultural varieties are raised from seed indoors;

---

* Named in honour of George Forrest, who collected in China. He was born at Falkirk in March, 1873 and died at Tengyueh on 5th January, 1932. He found this Primula in NW Yunnan. It is a fragrant species, about 9 inches tall, with orange-yellow flowers, with a deep orange eye.

successive sowings will give you Primulas in bloom all through the year. The winter temperature should be around 50°F. So you may have to bring the plants from the alpine house into the living-room on frosty nights.

Saussurea stella (star: from the shape of the leaves) is a strange-looking, though singularly attractive plant, with outstretched leaves (like the spokes of a wheel) over the pot or pan—often described as star-fish-like, but they are much thinner and longer than the lobes or rays of the star-fish. It is quite unlike any of the other thirty-odd species known and is regarded somewhat as a 'collector's piece'. The leaves make a star-shaped rosette; the largest are about 8 inches long; they are very narrow, leathery, deep glossy green in colour and marked purplish-red at the base. In the centre grow the thistle-like flowers an inch high, blue-purple in colour and surrounded by straw-coloured bristles. *Saussurea* have a wide distribution over the globe; our species, introduced in 1938, comes from the mountains of Tibet; in cultivation it needs perfect drainage, provided by 2 inches of limy rubble at the bottom of the pot, and a light loamy soil. It is quite hardy but its foliage is apt to be spoiled by wet and attacks by slugs in the open rock-garden.

Saxifrages grown in the alpine house are usually the Kabschia-Engleria plants, with stiff, silvery rosettes of leaves which are often pitted with white or silver lime. The reason is that the hot summer sun soon scorches up the leaves, and excessive rain in winter causes them to rot and damp off. Outside (in the scree) these plants need partial shade during the summer and overhead protection during the long winter months. Furthermore they are precocious flowerers and are covered with blossom as early as February—or they should be; but frost will quickly spoil the show. Without a doubt the best place for these lovely mat-forming Saxifrages is the alpine house, or the cold greenhouse.

First the *S. burseriana* group. They form large silvery cushions of rosettes that soon cover a pot or a pan with open little flowers on single stems 2 to 3 inches long. There are many fine varieties. Two of the loveliest are 'Gloria', with large white flowers on 2-inch red stems; and the exquisite lemon-yellow 'Sulphurea' whose flowers are borne on tiny pink stems. These Kabschias need limestone scree soil, limestone chippings round them and plenty of coarse drainage material at the bottom of their pots. The *burseriana** hybrid, *S.* × *jenkinsae*, forms tiny grey hummocks covered with multitudes of deep pink flowers on 1-inch stems. A charming plant for a pan—and in full bloom in February under glass. Watering must be done carefully: pour some water into a bowl and stand the pan in it till the soil and the roots are thoroughly moistened.

S. fortunei is an autumn-flowering species (native to China and Japan) that needs a partly-shaded place in summer and a warm, sheltered one in winter. For this reason it is often grown in pots under glass. The soil must be rich in humus and moisture retentive: use equal parts of loam (from the kitchen garden) and sifted leafmould or peat. It also makes a fine house plant for the autumn and is often brought into the living-room just before its flowers begin to open. The rather untidy-looking but charming clusters of white star-like flowers come at the end of tall fleshy stems (about 12 inches high); the leaves, large, round, leathery and glossy form attractive clumps which die down completely in winter. The best form is Wada's Variety, with leaves conspicuously crimson beneath. The plant costs about 35p.

Sedum spathulifolium 'Capablanca' is a fleshy, grey-leaved rosette plant almost covered with white farina that is often ruined by rain. To preserve it, and to keep the plant white and powdery-looking, grow it in a pot of gritty, light soil on a sunny shelf.

Thymus membranaceus is a shrubby, very fragrant Thyme from the rocky slopes of Spain and, like many of the shrubby kinds, gives a better show in a pot under glass, though this particular species has been grown very successfully on a sunny sheltered scree slope. The bracts, $\frac{1}{2}$ inch wide, are its most striking character: they are membranous (skin-like), greenish-white, sometimes pinkish, and surround the small, tubular pale lilac flowers, which are comparatively insignificant but give a touch of colour to the rounded little bush; it is about 6 inches high. All the Thymes prosper in a light loamy soil and like plenty of sun. Propagation of the shrubby kind is by cuttings in June.

* The specific epithet commemorates the scientific writer Joachim Burser, 1583–1649.

Verbascum have the name for spreading in the garden: they are almost as bad as the 'Welsh Poppy' (*Meconopsis cambrica*, page 28) and, like that plant, have been found in the wild growing and thriving on old walls, which indicates that they don't object to lime and chalk. All the species need well-drained soils containing lime. What is not so well known about the family is that it contains several species that are suitable for the rock-garden. Every gardener knows the tall perennial varieties with spikes of yellow flowers and whitish woolly leaves—the herbaceous-border 'Mulleins'.

The dwarf *V. dumulosum*, from South-West Turkey, where it is found growing on walls, is a rarity, a shrubby plant 12 inches high, with silvery-grey woolly leaves and small spikes of yellow flowers; another, even more rare, is *V. spinosum* from Crete; it has provided a very fine hybrid called 'Letitia'. This is the favourite Rock Verbascum for the alpine house. A little plant, 8 inches high, with silvery, woolly leaves 2 inches long and short racemes of yellow flowers with red-brown centres.

Some of these small, bushy Verbascums are recommended for growing in sink-gardens, which are described in the following chapter.

CHAPTER 6

Alpines in Sinks and Troughs

The kitchen sink sounds common enough and we might well wonder how it got into alpine-gardening. When did sink-gardening begin? (See our first sentence, page 9). Apparently much later than rock-gardening. The first sink-garden ingeniously and beautifully planted with rockery plants, was exhibited at the Royal Society's Chelsea Flower Show in 1923.* We can be sure of that date, because the object was on view. And from then onward sinks—the old-fashioned, shallow, stone-ones—have become increasingly popular with gardeners who have no room for a rockery, wall-garden, moraine or alpine house. And many live in towns and cities and have nothing worth calling a garden, perhaps nothing more than a small paved area enclosed by walls, against which a couple of trees or a few climbers are planted. For these people who specially want to grow rockery plants somehow and somewhere, the sink and the stone trough provide them with the means of doing so.

Two kitchen sinks are better than one—they might easily accommodate about thirty-odd alpines between them, perhaps more, depending on the size of the plants.

Before dealing with the preparation of the sink, filling it with soil, etc., let us first look at some of the other containers that have been used, such as pans, earthenware bowls and the like. It is well known that the Japanese were past-masters in the art of miniature gardening centuries ago, producing those famous dwarfed trees in glazed pots, and tiny gardens in trays. It is possible to buy these earthenware trays and pans. And they are

* Clarence Elliott, the collector and gardener, after experimenting with various receptacles (earthenware pans, etc.) seems to have hit upon the idea of using a sink for miniature gardens some years before the Chelsea exhibition mentioned here.

ideal for people who have no garden at all; they keep their plants indoors or use their window-sills. Sinks would be out of place in a living-room and much too big for a window-sill.

Another type of container is the stone trough, used for animals. This is larger than the sink but usually room can be found for one in the average-sized garden. You can plant in one trough (say, a pig trough) what you can plant in two sinks.

The least suitable objects are the highly ornamental or the elaborately carved receptacles and those made of polished metal. These are useful for holding a single shrub or a miniature evergreen tree. But alpines, whatever their habit (tufted, creeping or trailing) look out of place in them: they need rough, crude surfaces.

In passing, it is worth mentioning that sinks—the old stone ones measuring 2 foot 8 inches long by 1 foot 8 inches wide and about 5 inches deep—may be found in builders' yards and are sometimes offered for sale by alpine nurseries. Animal troughs are more difficult to come by but they are not so popular; and most gardeners prefer a couple of sinks, one fixed in a sunny place for plants that like full sun; the other in a semi-shady place for shade-loving plants. I say fixed advisedly, since if they are not cemented on to a pedestal or some sort of support, they might easily be overturned and the plants damaged.

Troughs are set up on four stone blocks as a rule, about 12 inches high; sinks usually on two stone supports, one at each end and extending the width of the sink; they are made of square blocks raised to a height of about 2 feet from the ground; at this height one can enjoy the plants and tend them more easily; moreover they will be safe from slugs, woodlice and other creeping pests. (*Campanula Zoysii* and *Thlaspi rotundifolium*, plants nearly always destroyed by slugs, are sometimes grown in sinks). Do not use bricks, which look out of place, for building the supports.

A sink always has an outlet hole, an inch from the back, in the right-hand corner; by slightly tilting the sink towards the outlet hole when you cement it in position on the supports, perfect drainage will be ensured. Troughs, however, have no outlet holes, so it will be necessary to cut them with a stonemason's chisel and hammer. An easy enough job. Before finally cementing the containers in position, pour water into them and watch its progress; it should drain away quickly and efficiently.

Cover the outlet holes with one or two large crocks and put some smaller ones over these. Then cover the bottom with biggish pebbles, rubble or very coarse gravel. The depth of this layer depends on the depth of the containers. Shallow sinks, which can be used only for plants that do not make long roots, will need about an inch or so of drainage material. Troughs which are comparatively deep, should be filled to one-third of their depth.

To prevent the top soil you add last of all from working down into the drainage material and clogging it, press fairly firmly on to it a layer of coarse, shredded peat or broken up leafmould.

At this stage it is necessary to put in position in the shallow sink-garden any miniature pieces of rock—weathered limestone preferably—if an outcrop effect or perhaps an alpine landscape effect is wanted. Press the soil round them to keep them firmly in place. In a trough, the rocks—larger pieces of course—may be arranged when it is three-quarters full of soil.

The soil to fill up with, should be a good gritty compost consisting of equal parts of fibrous loam and sifted leafmould or peat; one part coarse sand; and two parts of limestone or sandstone chippings, depending on the type of plants to be grown. In a trough garden, for instance, you could grow some of the creeping Rhododendrons if you wanted to, plants that will not tolerate lime in any form; for these, sandstone chippings would be used to keep the soil open and cool.

Tufa is an excellent rock for use in sinks and troughs. A miniature alpine plateau could be devised with sizeable pieces, in which holes can be bored, then filled with suitable soil and tiny alpines planted in them. Even lime-hating plants grow well in this soft calcareous rock.

Sink gardens stood in a sunny place quickly dry out, especially during a long hot summer spell and should therefore be watered daily. In a shady place or in partial shade the soil will retain its moisture very much longer; watering will be necessary probably only once a week or even less than that, depending of course on the weather. Troughs being larger, longer and deeper do not dry out so quickly. The best time for watering is late evening. Some plants, by the way, will need a pane of glass putting over them during the winter to protect their crowns and their downy foliage from wet and damp.

A matter worth mentioning here is that some sinks are used to accommodate one kind of plant only: a whole miniature Sedum garden, for instance; or a Saxifrage garden; a miniature forest, planted entirely with tiny conifers; a miniature alpine lawn; a wild garden; a water garden, with a tiny pool on which float one or two exiguous Water-lilies (*Nymphaea pygmaea alba* has white flowers about an inch wide); a miniature Daffodil garden. These miniature gardens give enormous pleasure to town and city dwellers who have no hope of ever owning any sort of garden anywhere. With fewer opportunities for cultivating gardens and less space available for them, they may well be the future gardens of thousands.

Most people like to have as many different kinds of plants as possible in their sinks and troughs. And there are plenty to choose from, as I have indicated above. There are the usual alpines— most people choose a mixture of them; bulbs and corms, such as the miniature Daffodils and tiny Cyclamen; trailing plants like the furry-leaved *Androsace lanuginosa*; these are allowed to trail over the side of the sink; carpeting plants: such as Sedums and Saxifrages; dwarf slow-growing trees, Conifers and Shrubs; water plants, chiefly the miniature Water-lilies. You might choose a dozen different kinds of alpines, or you might prefer to have one or two miniature trees, with some rare alpine carpeting the soil underneath them.

The important thing is that all the plants must be the smallest kinds, those that take up the least amount of room, the least bulky ones. They must not grow tall, not above a few inches in the case of the herbaceous kinds, and not spread far. We can't grow *Arabis, Aubrietia* and *Alyssum* in a sink-garden, or if we do, then only for a season; after one show we must dig them up and plant something else.

Several suitable plants we can call to mind immediately: *Arenaria balearica*, $\frac{1}{2}$ inch tall, with moss-like foliage and minute pin-head white flowers (page 100) is one; but it is invasive and would probably have to be pulled up after a year or two. That can be done quite easily and without damaging the plant; and it can be replanted in a cool moist place in the rockery. Similarly treated are the *Raoulia*, alpines from Australia and New Zealand; they are more difficult than the *Arenaria*; and it is something of a triumph if you can get them to succeed. Once they are established, it would be wise to leave them alone—grow them, or one of them, under or near a miniature conifer or some tiny evergreen tree in the sink-garden. It will provide an attractive plant association.

The half-inch or inch-high alpine plants are the ideal ones for sinks; above a few inches—certainly above 6 inches—they look out of place. Slightly taller plants are all right in the trough-garden.

Probably every herbaceous kind of alpine when grown in a sink, or some other smallish container, will need pruning back or cutting down to keep it within bounds. The effect of a trailer hanging over the side of a sink and down the stone supports would be incongruous and look absurd. Trailers in all types of containers must be pruned back regularly.

The plants that need the least attention and never need cutting back or pruning are the miniature trees and shrubs; some are evergreen, some deciduous; and there are flowering kinds and those whose flowers are inconspicuous and are grown specially for their foliage.

For beauty of foliage I recommend the Maples. Small plants can be bought in pots and for a sink-garden they may be left in their pots and sunk in the soil and grown like that for some years.

Acer is the name of the Maple family and it includes the gorgeous Japanese Maples noted for their magnificent autumn tints and also for their bright leaf colours—scarlet, yellow, green—in early spring. After many years of extremely slow growth, the plants do eventually reach shrub height. But you may safely leave a specimen in a sink or a trough untouched for a very long time. *Acer palmatum* is the famous plant that has provided us with so many lovely varieties. *A. palmatum dissectum aureum*, with finely divided (almost fern-like) leaves is a beauty; the colouring is first bright yellow, then deep gold. Another, with shining yellow foliage in spring, then deep butter yellow later, is *A. p. septemlobum lutescens*—its leaves are seven-lobed.

Plant these Japanese Maples near the end of the sink or the trough, and in rich, moist peaty or leafmould soil with an admixture of coarse sand. They are surface-rooting plants. And they give the best show in warm southern gardens. For the late spring frosts of colder places will often ruin the fresh young foliage as it begins to unfold. Around London they must have some overhead protection when a spring frost is imminent.

For a striking colour association in late autumn, grow the sky-blue *Gentiana sino-ornata* under or close to any of these Maples. The glowing orange, crimson and scarlet foliage of *Acer. p.s. osakazuki* is doubly beautiful with an underplanting of deep blue Gentians. Both plants like a lime-free, acid soil. Japanese Maples are on the expensive side.

Berberis suitable for sinks and troughs are modest-looking shrubs compared with the spectacular Maples just described, although one—the tall bushy *B. Thunbergii*—is as brilliantly coloured as any of the Maples. Several dwarf kinds have been recommended for sinks and troughs. I single out for any small sink-garden *B. Thunbergii atropurpurea nana* from Japan and not more than 12 inches high when fully grown. The foliage is constantly purple-red through the year, then turns a crimson-purple in autumn. Ordinary loamy soil suits this Berberis.

Betula nana (dwarf) is a Beech from the cold northern regions and among the hardiest of all trees. After many years it may reach a height of 12 inches or so; its leaves, tiny, glossy and rounded, turn yellow and gold before falling. It likes moist soils and will actually thrive in damp places; you need not worry about the soil in your sink or trough being wet with this little plant in it.

Cedrus libani 'Sargentii' is a miniature drooping Cedar—you can raise it from seed (as you can many shrubs and trees) and plant a seedling in your sink and probably in thirty years it won't have grown much above 12 inches. The drooping branches are clothed with needle-like leaves of an attractive glaucous green colour.

Jasminum Parkeri described on page 109 is a perfect little yellow-flowered shrublet for a sink. The brilliant blue spring Gentian looks magnificent against it; plant them fairly close together.

Juniper communis compressus has been called the perfect little evergreen conifer for a sink-garden. It is a remarkably slow-growing plant: you probably won't notice any difference in its size for many years. A dense, cone-shaped shrublet with tiny, sharp-pointed glaucous leaves. It thrives in limy, open soils. I think it looks best in a sink, planted against a largish piece of tufa rock. I have seen it growing actually in a deep cavity scooped out of a piece of tufa, half buried in loam in a trough.

Philesia magellanica (from the Magellan Archipelago) is an evergreen shrub, in cultivation reaching only a height of from 6 to 12 inches—in nature much taller and bigger. As it thrives only in partially-shady places, it must be planted in a sink or a trough stood somewhere out of the sun. It blooms in June, bearing tubular, rose-crimson flowers 2 inches long at the end of the stems, which are clothed with narrowish leaves, dark green above and glaucous beneath. Plant it in a well-drained leafy, lime-free soil, and give it some overhead protection during the winter months. It is probably only genuinely hardy in our warm seaside gardens.

Picea abies Gregoryana is another delightful miniature conifer. The type, *P. abies*, is the Christmas Tree, and our shrub (one of many varieties) is the best for a sink or a trough. It is a dense, cushion-shaped bushlet, with sharp needle-like leaves and is usually under 12 inches high; it needs a light, loamy moist soil and in its early stages of growth likes a place sheltered from high wind.

Pinus mugo pumilio is the tiniest Mountain Pine, sometimes called the European Scrub Pine and recommended not only for sinks and troughs but for any exposed position in the rock-garden. After some years it usually makes a squat, spreading bush 12 inches tall. Its many closely-set branches bear very attractive small cones.

P. sylvestris 'Beauvronensis', is rightly called the best of the miniature Pines. It is a dwarf, densely branched shrublet that takes many years to grow a few inches. *P. sylvestris nana* is another slow-growing dwarf; and *P.s. pumila* yet another—rounded in shape with short glaucous leaves. These Pines like fairly light well-drained loamy soils.

Rhododendrons are the most striking and the most floriferous of all the shrubs suitable for sinks and troughs. You can get them very small in pots, not much more than 6 inches tall when in full bloom. And they grow slowly. They are surface-rooting plants needing lime-free, peaty soil and perhaps some overhead protection during a late spring frost to preserve the flowers (see page 82 where several kinds are mentioned). The small-leaved kinds—belonging to the Lapponicum Series—are most suitable. R. *chryseum*, ultimately about 18 inches high, with bright yellow flowers an inch wide and small ovalish evergreen leaves, is an excellent choice. R. *scintillans* has lavender-blue flowers and is described by a local nursery as 'one of the best of all dwarf shrubs'. After many years it reaches a height of from 2 to 3 feet. Too tall then probably for a sink-garden; but like all Rhododendrons very easily moved and transplanted to the garden. The hybrids are considered to be tougher plants: there are many of them: 'Augfast' (blue, or mauvish-blue); 'Blue Bird' (violet-blue—see page 82); 'Carmine' (dark red); 'Intrifast' (another shade of blue); 'Treasure' (deep pink bell-shaped flowers) are some of the best. (Small specimens of these shrubs cost about £1 each.)

Rosa chinensis var. minima is the Fairy Rose described on page 27, and it and its many varieties are more at home perhaps in a sink-garden than in the rockery. 'Oakington Ruby', rather spreading, with tiny ruby-carmine flowers; and pink 'Rouletti', never above 6 inches high, go well together. An attractive miniature rose garden could be made by planting four or more of the same varieties in tiny formal beds measuring about 8 inches square. These tiny roses need plenty of sun and soil in good heart.

Salix are Willows; the big Weeping Willow, with its long, trailing yellow cord-like branches, being a favourite tree with most gardeners. Unfortunately there is no genuine dwarf resembling it. But there are several kinds suitable for the rockery and for sinks and troughs. *Salix herbacea* is a native plant, the smallest of all our wildings and a genuine shrub, not—as its name suggests—an herbaceous plant. It is never much above 4 inches high and makes an attractive tuft or carpet plant of tiny roundish leaves;

the catkins, about ¼ inch long, appear in April and colour the
plant golden-yellow. The stems creep over the ground, root there
and are often buried in the soil.

S. reticulata is another dwarf and an excellent choice for the
sink-garden. It seldom grows taller than 5 inches and forms a
patch of branching stems which will soon cover a good-sized
piece of tufa with attractive roundish leaves ½ inch across and
upright red-gold catkins in May.

Both species prosper in moist or even wet soil, such as the
tiny, white-flowered *Arenaria balearica* needs. If the sink-garden
is in a shady place, the latter creeper would make a good contrasting plant to grow with either of them.

Taxus are the Yews; and *Taxus baccata* (with fleshy berries) is
the English Yew or Common Yew, famous for its intense dark
green, almost black-green foliage. Against it, flowering plants of
all kinds show up remarkably well. Dwarf Yews can be similarly
used in a sink-garden. But one important thing must be remembered: they will not live long in waterlogged soil. Never let the
soil become too wet. It must be thoroughly well drained and
should slope down to the centre of the sink. It can be built up
and partly supported by good-sized pieces of limestone rock.
Set the Yew or Yews at the top quite near the stone edge and
the other plants in front. The miniature Yews can be: *Taxus
baccata pygmaea* the smallest of the dwarfs: a rounded little bush
very suitable for a sink-garden; *Var. nana*, another little bush,
compact, with dark green, glossy leaves, which takes many years
to grow an inch; *Var. nutans*, a dense, compact bush with tiny
leaves; *Var. repandens*, a low growing, wide-spreading dwarf,
which makes a perfect background plant.

In front of these dwarf Yews any of the small flowering alpines,
or those with greyish-silver foliage, stand out more conspicuously
than when planted on their own somewhere or against a rock.

One of the favourite flowering plants for a sink is the small
Campanula cochlearifolia var. alba, with tiny pure white bells, which
against a Yew gives a striking black-and-white effect. It is however an invasive plant and its underground stems need pulling up
when they spread too far. Another half a dozen species have been
recommended, all tiny plants but most of them inclined to spread

rather quickly. Several kinds are mentioned in Chapter 2. A special favourite of mine is *C. garganica hirsuta var. alba*, about 4 inches tall, with grey-downy foliage and pure white bells. Plant it against one of the Yews.

Many of the plants described in the preceding chapters may be grown in sinks or troughs. The exceptions are: those that are on the tender side and are best grown permanently under glass; those that creep too far, such as *Cerastium tomentosa*; very vigorous trailers, and those that grow taller than 6 inches or so.

Androsace lanuginosa is a charming little trailer for a sink-garden; plant it in a pocket of light, leafy, gritty soil near the edge and let the stems grow over the side. It has silvery hairy foliage and small heads of tiny pink Verbena-like flowers, with a yellow eye; the white variety is described in Chapter 3. Both bloom through the summer months.

Asperula lilaciflora caespitosa is another summer trailer; it forms a mat of deep glossy green, heather-like leaves, from which come the star-shaped deep carmine-pink flowers on inch-long stems. (Gritty, well-drained leafy soil and plenty of sun for it.)

Linum salsoloides, a June-flowering plant, recommended for a sink or a trough; train its stems (6 to 8 inches long) over the sides; the terminal sprays of pearly-white flowers with purple centres contrast well with the tiny evergreen, narrow leaves.

Phlox douglassi 'May Snow' is a lovely white-flowered trailer for a sink; another variety is 'Rose Queen', with silvery-rose flowers. And *Phlox subulata* 'Temiscaming', has deep red-purple flowers and is considered the finest of the *subulata* group. These alpine Phloxes are vigorous plants and will need cutting back after a season. Give them leafy-gritty soil and protect them from the scorching sun.

Arenaria balearica is a good carpeting plant but invasive. Another species is *A. tetraquetra*, with tightly-packed, formal-looking leaves and white flowers borne on stems 2 inches high.

Other carpeters more choice are *Raoulia lutescens* (page 30); *R. glabra*, more green in appearance; the very beautiful *Sedum album* 'Coral Carpet', with coral-pink foliage and pink flowers on 2-inch stems.

And some shrubby plants recommended for the trough-garden

—they are rather too tall for a sink—include the best forms of the Heather, *Erica carnea*, such as 'Eileen Porter', with glowing pink flowers in February; 'King George', dark red; 'Queen Mary', rose-pink; 'Winter Beauty', another deep pink—it's usually in bloom by Christmas. They all like leafy, sandy soil and thrive where there is lime, unlike many Heathers that prefer peaty, acid soils found on sand or lime-free rocks. *Verbascum spinosum* (see the preceding chapter for other kinds) is recommended by the R.H.S. Dictionary for growing in a sink; it reaches a height of about 9 inches. It's a curiously attractive shrubby plant from Crete, with slender grey branchlets armed with terminal spines; the leaves are narrow, downy and greyish-green; and the flowers, of an attractive yellow colour, come in short spikes. It likes full sun, a well-drained leafy, gritty soil and protection during long wet spells.

The various miniature gardens referred to on page 150 need their own special kinds of plants—flat or creeping or mat-forming plants for the alpine lawn; and the tiniest Water-lilies for the miniature pool. The smallest are *Nymphaea* × *pygmaea helvola* (primrose-yellow flowers); *N. pygmaea alba* (white); *N. tetragona* (white and sometimes scented). The pool for a sink-garden may be a formal one, that is, circular or rectangular, or free and quite informal. Nowadays small plastic bowls or pool-shapes can be bought from many horticultural stores; one about 10 inches across and 6 inches deep would be big enough for two of the smallest plants, such as those described above. Put a layer 3 inches deep of fibrous, leafy loam at the bottom; plant the roots or rhizomes very firmly in this—a couple of stones will help to keep them in position—then add about an inch and a half of rain-water; as the leaves grow, add more and finally fill the pool completely. The best time for planting is May, when the water will get quickly warmed. And the plants need plenty of sun.

CHAPTER 7

Pathways and Steps

Paving plants look best on stone; and usually out of place on brick. Moreover brick paths are mostly patterned—the fish-bone pattern is popular—and therefore sufficiently attractive without the addition of plants. Not of course that stone is unattractive. Yorkshire flagstones laid in well mown grass in a formal part of a garden are cool-looking and picturesque. They may be used in wilder parts: for paving in woodland; through a rockery; for a pathway along the base of a wall-garden; though I think the self-faced (undressed) stone with its uneven surface is more in keeping with wilder places, especially where alpines grow.

The paving-stone for a woodland walk should be the undressed natural stone. This is usually advertised as 'Rectangular Paving'; a favourite variety is the new self-faced York stone slabs, random sizes 1 to 2 inches thick, approximately 12 square yards to a ton, buff (dull yellow) at £3·25. It looks attractive anywhere in the wild-garden or in the rockery and is as good as any you can get. There are thicker grades, approximately seven square yards to a ton—buff-grey at £1·75. Hortex pre-cast paving slabs in eight sizes, 1½ inches thick are cheaper at £1·13 a ton.

The width of a path depends usually on the size of the garden and on the amount of room one is prepared to use for it. A landscape gardener of my acquaintance states: 2 feet 6 inches for a single file; twice that width for two people to walk abreast in comfort.

Where there is a woodland, no doubt there would be room for the wider path. The rockery pathway (in the dell—see page 21), and the path along the foot of a wall-garden could be narrower, say, 3 feet wide; though again, this depends on the space available: a large, wide dell could have a pathway through it 4 feet wide. Whatever its width, whatever its length, the path must lead somewhere; it must be practicable and direct.

Mostly a layer of ashes or sand 3 or 4 inches deep (well rolled down) is used for the foundation. Personally I also like to spread a thinnish layer of fairly liquid cement over the ashes to keep the slabs firmly and permanently in position and to prevent weeds from springing up through the joints after a season or two. It will be necessary of course to remove with a sharp pointed trowel the wet cement and the ashes from the joints or crevices in which plants are to be grown. These crevices should be about 2 inches wide and filled with good deep loamy soil.

Woodland paths should not be regular or formal in their design as are the main stone or concrete pathways that lead to and from the house and other buildings. Here and there use half slabs and smaller pieces to vary the width. If you can't break the biggest pieces neatly, get the stone-mason to do it for you.

The easiest way to plant the path is to sow seeds in the crevices. But before doing this, find out when the path gets most sun on it. Being a woodland path, it probably doesn't get very much. And no doubt most of the plants will have to be those that flourish in shade and perhaps in sunless places. The well known and invasive *Arenaria balearica* is one; it will probably need pulling up every so often when it begins to spread.

Our native Primrose flowers freely and looks well in the crevices of a woodland path; the common yellow *Primula vulgaris* is perhaps more suitable than the vividly-coloured varieties. Primroses are easily raised from seed; sow them in April or May in the crevices where you want them to bloom; thin out the seedlings to about 4 inches apart when they are big enough, leaving those you want undisturbed. The variety *P. vulgaris sibthorpii*, with pale pink or lilac flowers, makes a good companion for the common sort. Both should be planted in the woodland, too, drifting down to the edge of the path. The 'Drum-stick Primula', *P. denticulata* (page 80), is another good plant for a shady pathway. Sow the seed in a crevice and some in the woodland.

Many of the Mossy Saxifrages will grow and flower well on the sunnier parts of a paved walk. *Saxifraga caespitosa*, with leaves in dense green tufts and small white flowers 3 inches high, is a choice crevice plant for partial shade and needs gritty, moist soil. And the miniature forms of 'London Pride' (*S. umbrosa*) are ideal for woodland paths. *S. umbrosa* 'Elliott's Form', with small green leaves and tiny, deep pink flowers, 4 inches high, is especially recommended.

If you can establish these plants in the crevices, it is certain that they will grow well in the adjoining woodland. The soil there is naturally leafy and suitable for most shade-loving things. Varieties of 'London Pride' may also be grown along both sides of the woodland pathway to cover up unsightly edges. The type, *Saxifraga umbrosa* is 12 inches tall: too tall for a crevice in the middle of the path, but all right at the side and should be allowed to encroach on the pathway to give the effect of wild, natural growth spilling out from the woodland. Among the best of the edging plants is the soft, semi-trailing 'Foam Flower', *Tiarella cordifolia*. This is a dwarfish plant, a native of Eastern North America, which spreads and partly trails or falls by means of stolons or runners (like the Strawberry plant) and has heart-shaped lobed leaves (the biggest 4 inches long) and clusters of feathery, white flowers—resembling foam in the mass—on 9-inch stems. It gives a soft, pretty effect in the subdued light of a woodland and must be grown in shade and in moist leafy soil, though it prospers well in ordinary garden loam. It spreads quickly and is useful in a large woodland garden. It looks lovely hanging over a shady step.

The large-leaved Ivies are also excellent edging plants and grow luxuriantly in woodlands and will spread quickly out on to a pathway. Try the so-called 'Persian Ivy', *Hedera colchia*, which has ovalish or heart-shaped leaves often 8 inches long and 4 inches wide, of a lustrous dark green: a handsome, vigorous creeping plant that has given us one or two very attractive varieties—the variegated form is the best, I think.

Hedera hibernica, the 'Irish Ivy' (found wild in Ireland and Scotland) has big leaves, 6 inches wide, very dark green in colour; it is one of the best of all evergreen carpeting plants for shady places and, it should be noted, does well where the soil is quite thin. The variety *maculata* has attractive leaves marked yellow and white. A very attractive variety of the common Ivy *Hedera*

Rock garden showing water flowing through (artificial); dwarf Junipers in the background; *Genista delphinensis* in the foreground.

Aubrietia 'Crimson Queen', a favourite carpeting plant for a sunny spot in the rockery.

Mimulus (Monkey Musk), a striking little plant for a moist sunny spot.

helix, is *digitata*, with largish leaves divided into finger-like lobes. These leaves are beautifully conspicuous spread out flat over the edge of the stone pathway. And the tiny variety *minima*, with leaves ½ inch across, could be grown actually on the path, in a crevice of deep leafy soil.

Ivies do best in shade; 'Periwinkles' (*Vinca*), on the other hand, don't mind sun or shade; they are valued as undergrowth in woods and spread fairly rapidly. *Vinca major* is the best known kind. Its blue-purple open flowers are attractive but not very showy.

Grow the hardy Fern *Athyrium felix-foemina* (the 'Lady Fern') with it and with the 'Foam Flower'; Ferns are excellent foil plants. This species is about 3 feet tall and has graceful light green fronds. And the tiniest ones such as *Adiantum venustum*, and the creeping *Cystopteris montana*, if you can manage them, are quite at home in the cool crevices of a woodland pathway.

It is worth while to mention here that the Heather-path was at one time common in many woodland gardens. Diverse kinds of Heathers were used; but the Scotch Heather, *Calluna vulgaris*, a white-flowered evergreen shrubby plant, was the favourite sort; it was mown over regularly to keep it short and to make a walkable pathway of it. The double variety *C. vulgaris alba plena*, a smaller plant, about half the height of the other was also used and I imagine more easily mown. Readers might like to try these plants, if their soils are lime-free. Both must have a peaty, sandy soil free from any trace of lime or chalk to grow in. And it is better to be on the thin, starved side than rich and deep, otherwise the plants will grow tall and gaunt and soon become woody-stemmed and hard to cut.

Pathways in rockeries and along the bottom of a wall-garden are nearly always made of crazy paving, which, however well and skilfully laid, never equals in appearance good quality York paving stone or the best flagstones. (The term 'crazy' is apparently from 'Crazy-quilt'.) The paving consists of irregularly-sized pieces of concrete put together rather in the same way that one forms a completed jig-saw puzzle—though as a rule there are no curved or rounded pieces.

The method of laying it is the same as for flagstones and for the woodland described above.

Scoop out the cement and ashes from the crevices where plants are to be grown. But there is a tendency, it seems, to fill practically every crevice with some kind of plant. And the resulting overgrowth is anything but pleasing to the eye. Too much overgrowth is always ugly and usually gets more treading upon than the paving-stone itself. There are a great number of alpines however that can be walked on without suffering any damage and they have sufficient resilience to resume their normal shape almost immediately. Heather—especially the small mat-forming kinds—withstand a great deal of hard wear. The 'Cheddar Pink' is another very tough mat-forming plant that doesn't mind being walked upon when not in flower.

Mat-forming, flattish plants are the best for growing in the crevices or interstices of paved walks. And as most rock-gardens and wall-gardens are built in sunny places, the plants chosen for the crevices of the paths will be those that revel in plenty of sun.

Several kinds have been described in Chapter 2. Many gardeners prefer to grow them in the crevices of rocks and boulders because high up these plants are seen to best advantage. And many people moreover have gravel or sanded pathways, which of course are unsuitable for most carpeting or mat-forming alpines.

Acaena, belonging to the Rose family (*Rosaceae*), are excellent plants for crazy paving. *A. sanguisorbae*, with minute light green, briar-like foliage is probably the loveliest for a stone path; see page 40.

Antennaria belong to the Daisy family (closely allied to the Edelweiss) and are grey mat-forming plants prized by alpine enthusiasts for covering sunny boulders and for growing in the crevices of crazy paving; one variety is described in Chapter 2; a special favourite for the crevices of a stone pathway is *Antennaria dioica minima*, the smallest of them all, only an inch high, with very woolly grey leaves.

Campanula cochlearifolia seems to grow well everywhere—on walls, in the rock-garden proper, in sinks, and in pots. There are three well known kinds, viz. the blue-flowered type; the white *alba*; and 'Miss Willmott', with larger, grey-blue bells. They all flourish in the crevices of a sunny, or partially shady stone pathway. They spread rapidly but are not difficult to control. Most of the low-growing species and varieties of Campanulas are suitable for growing on paved walks; they bloom longer in partial shade.

Corydalis lutea (yellowish) is a native plant, with narrow-lipped yellow flowers on tallish stems and finely divided delicate-looking leaves. Its flowers open in May and bloom intermittently all through the summer. It's a valuable plant for a crevice, grows well in light, loamy soils, in sun or shade, and has been known to settle (by seed) on gravel paths and thrive there. Some gardeners consider it too tall (12 inches) for a narrow path and use it as an edging plant. It is easily increased by seed and usually throws plenty of seedlings where it grows.

Cotula squalida (untidy, dingy) is described by Hillier as 'A carpeter with frond-like leaves. With *Acaena*, one of the best and most reliable plants for paving.' A charming, mat-forming plant from New Zealand with fern-like leaves on longish, creeping stems, which get rather untidy after a time, and inconspicuous, uninteresting purplish flowers. It needs pruning back from time to time and grows well in ordinary garden soil. It is easily increased by rooted pieces.

Dianthus (Pinks) are very popular for growing in crazy paving. Their leaves are evergreen and form attractive mats of often grey-green or glaucous foliage that are particularly good to see during the winter months. Our native 'Cheddar Pink' is a perfect crevice plant; so are its two varieties 'Baker's Variety', with big, deep pink flowers; and 'Flore Pleno', a rose coloured semi-double, very fragrant Pink. Plant them in sun or partial shade; cut off the dead flower-heads; and the plants won't mind being trodden on occasionally.

Dryas octopetala minor is half the size (in all its parts) of the type described in Chapter 2; and it doesn't spread so far; its tiny leaves, dark green above and grey below, make a charming mat for a sunny paved walk.

Erigeron mucronatus is recommended for wall-gardens and sometimes for crazy paving. It is not completely hardy in all districts and should be planted in a sheltered spot at the edge of a sunny path but not on it, where it might be too exposed to frost and snow.

Globularia are very suitable for paving. Several species are offered by nurseries; the best, *G. bellidifolia*, is a neat, densely tufted plant with numerous tiny wedge-shaped leaves and small heads of blue-grey flowers on tiny stems an inch high. *G. incanescens* has glaucous leaves and violet-blue flowers on 2-inch stems. These paving plants like a light limy soil and sunny dry places.

Gypsophila repens var. rosea is the branching, spreading plant, with tiny pink flowers, that is widely grown on rockeries and wall-gardens. The variety *fratensis* is the one recommended for paved walks; it is similar to the other, but of denser habit and has attractive reddish stems.

Irises, which are very dwarf—not above 4 or 5 inches tall—are excellent plants for growing in the crevices of crazy paving. A special place must be prepared for them: a widish crevice filled with deep leafy sandy soil. Grow either *Iris mellita* (4 inches tall), with smoky-brown flowers veined with red; or *I. pumila* or one of its varieties, with blue or yellow flowers. These plants, with their stiff sword-shaped leaves and largish flowers, are remarkable for the contrast they provide.

Raoulia, rare carpeting plants from New Zealand, are recommended for paved walks. They are however rather difficult in cultivation. *R. lutescens* (becoming yellow) makes a close mat of minute greyish leaves almost covered in summer with tiny stem-less lemon-yellow flowers. Best as a side or edge plant, in perfectly-drained leafy, gritty soil (see page 30). *R. australis* is a creeping mat of tiny silver rosettes and white flowers ($\frac{1}{2}$ inch high); and *R. glabra*, a green-leaved carpeter with tiny yellow flower clusters. To establish them in some rockeries, gardeners often cover them with handlights during bad weather—they are however completely hardy.

Saxifraga, Sedum and *Sempervivum* all provide suitable plants for stone pathways. Of the Saxifrage family, the miniature forms of the 'London Pride' are recommended; they are very adaptable; an important thing to remember, though, is that the variegated ones, such as *S. umbrosa variegata aurea*, should be planted in full sun for the sake of the leaf colouring.

Sedum thrive on rocks and stones, and *Sedum acre* (page 87), with its little bright yellow flowers, is a charming, though invasive plant for a stone path. *S. spathulifolium purpureum*, with its thick, fleshy leaves covered with a fruity bloom, is another and a beauty.

Sempervivum are best grown as side plants, established first in a very little rich loamy soil and allowed to spread on to the path. Perhaps the small rosette kinds are best. I personally like *S. allionii* with downy rosettes an inch across, pale green in colour and tipped with red.

Thymes are like Heathers—hard-wearing and don't mind being trodden on occasionally when they're not in flower. *Thymus drucei* has given us an astonishing number of varieties for decorating paved walks in sunny places. (See Chapter 2.) The plants are more fragrant when they are warmed by the sun and damped by the summer rains. *Thymus drucei var. coccineus*, a mat of rich crimson flowers, an inch high, is lovely spreading out over crazy paving. The grey-green flat, woolly *Thymus pseudolanuginosus*, usually flowerless, is often seen on paved walks and growing amongst other Thymes in the alpine lawn.

Steps, like retaining walls, need a special site. The slope is ideal for both (see Chapter 3, page 95). It is necessary in order to form a bank (if there is no natural bank) in which rocks are embedded to make a retaining wall. And steps are cut in the soil, since they are often easier to walk up than the slope itself, especially when it is frozen over and slippery. But when it comes to making a suitable site, the difficulties are often enormous. You can make a low retaining wall by first excavating soil to form a sunk garden adjacent to the house (a lengthy job) and at the same time have a few steps leading up to a terrace or a veranda adjoining the house.

Once you've got the sunk garden, you can go ahead and cut out the steps in the soil. And this is done of course on a slope. If the soil is clayey, you simply cut out the steps to the size you want them and form a core, which is to be cemented over first by a crude foundation layer and then by the smooth finishep surface. Loose, light soil will need supporting by a wooden mould.

There are several ways of making or building the steps. The easiest and the most popular is to use stone slabs (obtainable from any stone-mason's) 2 feet 6 inches long by 8 inches wide and 1 inch thick for level treads, cementing these firmly in position on concrete or rubble foundations. The tread (the step itself) can be much wider—it can go back much farther; on a gentle slope (the best sort of slope for steps) it could be 12 inches or more; and the 'risers' (the vertical height of the steps) need be only a few inches high. For the wider treads use two slabs (of the dimensions given above) and leave a crevice at the back for plants. The two together will give a tread of about 18 inches. The 'risers' are often bricks laid lengthways. Three will give an overall length of 2 feet 2 inches or so. They should be laid with their narrow sides (2½ inches high) showing outward; for a taller step, use a double layer, cementing the joints and leaving a small open crevice at the end, in which to plant an alpine that doesn't spread too far. Cement or concrete blocks, larger than bricks are obtainable (size: 12 by 4 by 2½ inches); these are excellent for making steps and you can get them from a stone-mason or a builder.

The sides, triangular bare pieces of soil, are usually covered by the stems of prostrate plants grown on the sloping ground running above the steps. Or broken slabs may be embedded in the soil to form small 'dry' triangular walls, in which plants may be grown.

I remember seeing dwarf Lavenders, *Santolina* ('Lavender Cotton') and *Artemisia* growing on sloping banks bordering long flights of stone steps. The 12-inch tall Lavender, *Lavendula Munstead Dwarf*, with deep purple flowers, earlier than the taller 'Old English', is an excellent shrubby plant for a bank and is charming grown with the *Santolina*. The latter is a rather untidy plant, at least after a couple of years, making long straggling growths and leaving the centre open and flat. The foliage and stems are felted and silvery-white in colour. The small, round, bright yellow flowers, which come in late summer, rather spoil the appearance of the plant and are best snipped off with the shears. Lavender and Santolina both need sandy soils on the light side and plenty of sun; the latter produces better coloured foliage—more intensely white—on poor, starved ground. *Arte-misias* are described in Chapter 2. Most of this family are shrubby, silvery-white foliage plants and will succeed where Lavender and Santolina grow. Their leaves when bruised, like those of the Santolina, are usually fragrant. All three are easily increased by cuttings. The *Santolina* is best replaced by new young plants every second year.

An herbaceous plant often used on a sunny sloping bank, one to trail down and reach the steps—if you want it to—is the 'Catmint', *Nepeta* × *faassenii* (often described in catalogues under the name of *N. mussini*, which is a different and on the whole less attractive plant). It is well known with its silver-grey leaves and hanging spikes of lavender-mauve flowers which bloom from about May to September. It looks singularly beautiful massed in front of the dark purple dwarf Lavender *Munstead Dwarf*. This 'Catmint' thrives in a light, sandy soil and likes sunny places. It is increased in spring by division or by cuttings.

Plants recommended for growing in the crevices of steps are those of compact habit, and, according to some gardeners, sub-dued in colour: pale blue, pink, blue-grey, lavender (what are known as pastel shades) being more in keeping with the formal character of the stonework than bright vivid colours.

Campanulas are some of the first plants that come to mind: there are plenty of compact kinds that don't spread too far; most can be kept in neat little clumps close against the steps and they are not too showy and never look out of place. *Campanula cochleari-folia*, which we have mentioned several times, is inclined to ramp with its underground, running stems, but is easily controlled when planted in a corner crevice of a step; it makes a neat clump of tiny nodding bellflowers—pale blue, grey-blue or white.

The most popular of all the Campanulas, *C. portenschlagiana*, with mauvish-blue bells, is often seen fringing the bottom steps. An unbroken mass or fringe of flowers is easily obtained by planting small rooted pieces of suitable alpines in crevices spaced, say, 6 inches apart.

Less obtrusive than this bellflower are the *Minuartias* (often listed in catalogues as *Arenarias*); *Minuartia verna* is the 'Spring

Sandwort', a small, mat-forming plant with tiny, narrow bright green leaves and clusters of white flowers on thread-like stems 3 inches high. It blooms from June to September. And *M. verna caespitosa* 'Aurea' is a charming crevice plant with moss-like mats of yellowish-green foliage. I've seen both growing well on steps, stone paving and in sink-gardens.

CHAPTER 8

Alpine Lawns

The chalet gardens high up in the Swiss Alps are wild gardens and never cultivated. Those on the grassy slopes below the upper peaks at Arosa in the Engadine are scythed over in the autumn, the grass and flowers raked up into heaps and made into hay. The great attraction of these little gardens is their perpetual freshness: the moist, green grass in midsummer and the tall-growing flowers, fresh and lovely from spring to autumn.

In England we don't get such gardens, for the simple reason we don't have the right sort of climate for them. Our wild flowers never grow so luxuriantly as the grass; and round about August the grass usually dries up, turns yellow and dies and the flowers seem to disappear. The only successful wild gardens are those we plan and make ourselves. And the alpine lawn, which is usually planned as part of a rock-garden, is a comparatively modern and popular type of wild garden.

If you have built a low dry wall (by excavating soil), you may have planted a lawn, which the wall partly surrounds, and which has to be mown every so often. Instead of the grass, plant suitable alpines to make an alpine lawn which will require little or no maintenance, certainly no mowing—unless you have a Heather pathway or walk running through it and mow that; a Scotch Heather walk was described in the previous chapter (page 161).

Grass must be rigorously weeded out. Possibly—as it grows practically anywhere—keeping it down or getting rid of it will be the most difficult job. As soon as a blade is seen, it must be dug up. Close planting of suitable alpines will however keep it out, perhaps permanently. (I have a Heather patch where grass hasn't been seen for twenty years.)

If the site chosen is that where a wall-garden has been made,

169

by excavating the soil, deep digging will have been done very efficiently, drainage will be perfect and all perennial weeds will have been removed. On the other hand, if the site is a level piece of ground where a rockery has been built, with rocks and boulders sunk a little into the soil, no doubt grass and weeds will be flourishing here and there. The soil must be dug over thoroughly and deeply and every scrap of vegetation removed; this is best done in the autumn so that the soil can be exposed to the weather and left to settle.

We can begin planting the following spring. What should be grown in an alpine lawn? First we must consider the position of the adjacent rocks—the rocks and boulders in the background. When we are substituting an alpine lawn for an ordinary grass lawn, where there is a low retaining wall partly covered with trailing alpines, we must grow within a foot of the wall only the shortest, mat-forming plants we can find, so that the wall face is not hidden. Alpines two or three feet tall would be quite out of place here obviously, especially if they were evergreens such as Heathers: you wouldn't see what was trailing down the wall. Even if there is a stone pathway running along the foot of the wall, it would be best to grow mat-forming alpines along it; taller plants—nothing taller than about 12 inches though—may be grown farther back in the lawn.

Secondly there is the nature of the soil to be considered. Perfectly-drained, ordinary garden soil is ideal for many of the plants we grow; but if it contains lime, it is quite unsuitable for Heathers (*Erica*) which like peaty, acid soils. These are probably among the first plants we think of, since most of us have tramped over Heather-covered moors in different parts of the country. They don't suffer through being walked upon. And it is wise of course to grow these toughish things in alpine lawns. In the wild, Heathers flourish in fibrous peat over a thin layer of sand and stones; in cultivation they mostly get soil that is too rich for them and consequently grow rank and thin. Start them off in a mixture of three parts of sifted leafmould or peat to one of washed sand and mulch them every spring with a layer of finely sifted leafmould 3 or 4 inches deep. Clip them over lightly with the shears after the flowering season to keep them reasonably low and bushy. The best kinds are the *Erica carnea* varieties, dwarf plants, not more than about 9 inches tall, winter blooming and lime tolerant. (See page 178.) Don't walk on them when they are in flower and clip them over at the end of April.

It has been said that an alpine lawn can consist of two plants only, viz. Heather and Thyme. Species of both families are found wild in the U.K. and the plants may be walked on without doing them any damage. The dwarf, mat-forming Thymes (*Thymus*) are best for our purpose. These are described in Chapter 2. *Thymus drucei* (some of them listed under *T. serphyllum*) are a group recommended by nurseries. 'Small leaved creeping plants (an inch high) forming close mats, which are ideal ground covers for chalky places. All are sheeted with blossom throughout the summer; they form miniature lawns, like patchwork quilts.'

Most spread out into mats about 12 inches or more across and should therefore be planted at least 12 inches apart. The lovely, spongy, grey-green species *T. pseudolanuginosus* (page 90), which seldom produces any flowers in this country, is $\frac{1}{2}$ inch high and a perfect carpeter for edging an alpine lawn or indeed if you like it well enough for covering the whole area—a fragrant Thyme lawn. And grow it with the flowering kinds and with any of the dwarf Heathers, for it will creep along and fill up any empty spaces. It is delightfully scented: a sweeter purer scent than the others. I've seen it thriving in all sorts of soils; it likes a chalky, light, sandy loam and is perhaps at its poorest in clay, which, anyway, isn't suitable for alpine lawns. And it prospers in leafy soil which most Heathers need.

Many gardeners use it as an underplanting for spring-flowering bulbs and corms. One could devote a whole chapter to the virtues of this soft spongy, pale green foliage Thyme.

Before considering some of the bulbous plants which we grow to break up the flattish expanse of foliage on the lawn, let us look at a few more suitable carpeters. Many have been described in Chapter 2.

Next in popularity to the Thymes apparently is the Chamomile (page 49). *Anthemis nobilis* (grand) is our plant: the 'Common Chamomile', used in the past for making Chamomile lawns and Chamomile tea; the flowers are daisy-like, white with a yellow centre and not very striking or grand; the leaves, finely divided and fern-like, are downy and form a spreading mat of bright green about 15 inches across. Its height is about 6 inches; the plant associates well with any of the carpeting Thymes. It thrives in sunny places, in a lightish, sandy soil; and is easily increased by division or by cuttings.

Acaena (page 39) are among the more rare carpeting plants and have small fern-like leaves and burr-like fruits in autumn. Recommended especially for paving. Most are about 2 inches high. Excellent too as an underplanting for spring bulbs and Anemones which push their way up through the bronze-green or grey-green foliage. Plant these *Acaena* 2 feet apart.

Asarum are wild-garden carpeting plants that do best in moist, shady places. If your alpine lawn is near water—as some are—you should grow the two species offered; see the end of the chapter.

Astilbe flourish in similar places and make fine contrasting plants set in an alpine lawn or patch near a stream.

Cotula squalida is recommended by alpine nurseries as a good carpeter with frond-like leaves. (Chapter 7) It spreads out into a dense, flat carpet about 24 inches across after a time and is often grown as an edging round a pond. An excellent ground cover for spring-flowering bulbs.

Dianthus gratianopolitanus, the Cheddar Pink, is sometimes used in the alpine lawn as a mat plant for the sake of its blue-grey foliage in winter; but it is not a dense mat; grass often begins to grow up through it. Well worth growing, however, for its foliage and its small very fragrant Pinks in summer.

Gentians one expects to see in an alpine lawn, and they are common enough in the Alps. But some are practically impossible to establish in cultivation. *Gentiana verna* is the one we see up in the Swiss chalet gardens, spreading freely in the short, spring grass. It has been tried in the alpine lawn but has never been much of a success. You might sink a pot or two of it in the soil and put tiny stone chips round the plants to completely hide the pots. I've seen this done near a patch of the grey-green woolly carpeting Thyme: three pots sunk along one side of it. You can't of course expect much of a show from a few pots and it seems that the only reliable Gentian for the alpine lawn is the Chinese *G. sino-ornata* described in Chapter 2. It forms spreading mats of evergreen rosettes from which the sky-blue trumpet flowers grow on 4-inch stems. You may walk lightly on the plants in early spring, and after they have finished flowering; but they are not so tough as Heathers and Thymes. Wonderful plants to grow in association with dwarf Heathers (in the background); both like the same sort of acid, peaty, lime-free soil.

Phlox douglassi and its varieties are fine patch or 'island' plants for a lawn where the soil is reasonably moist, well drained, and on the light side. Plant them near the later blooming Thymes to get a succession of flowers from May to late August.

Phlox douglassi 'Boothman's Variety' (2 inches tall) has clear mauve flowers with darker centres; 'May Snow' is a pure white carpeter; and 'Rose Queen' is a charming silvery-rose colour. These plants each have a spread of about 18 inches. The *Phlox subulata* varieties are equally useful for providing patches of colour.

Raoulia are usually grown in the interstices of paved walks (see Chapter 7). They are excellent too for lawns, forming green, or silver, or greyish mats of tight foliage ½ inch high. As they resent excessive moisture on them, they should be sprinkled with very coarse sand when they are first planted: too much wet soaking into the foliage often causes them to damp off. R. *australis*, silver foliage; and R. *glabra*, dark green smooth leaves are the two species recommended for the alpine lawn.

Stachys lanata 'Silver Carpet' is the non-flowering 'Lamb's Tongue', forming a 3-inch high carpet of silver-grey, soft woolly leaves and stems. It is a fine contrasting foliage plant for the lawn and likes well-drained, lightish soil in a sunny place.

Vinca minor 'Alba' is the white-flowered 'Periwinkle', which sends out longish rooting stems that form close mats of light green leaves; it is a valuable plant, since it does well in sun or shade and is not at all particular about the soil you give it. I have found it a useful evergreen carpeter for an alpine lawn; it is the only variety I grow; but there are others, more striking, with blue or with purplish flowers.

In all gardens these dwarf spreading Vincas don't always bloom very freely—mine: *Vinca minor* 'Alba' doesn't, because it's planted in a shady place—and these plants may then be used, as mine is, for an underplanting; common wood Anemones (*Anemone nemorosa*, page 47) grow up thickly through it. It's rather a dull bit of planting, with a few white Periwinkle flowers below the white Anemones. The deep blue *A. blanda* is a better choice to grow underneath the white *Vinca*. Many of the woodland Anemones make fine contrasting plants for the alpine lawn, though one must be careful to choose those of the right height for the mat-plants they are to adorn. And those, like the ones mentioned here that die down completely after blooming, are the best; for the flat lawn plants then resume their normal appearance; and anyhow the dead flower-heads and fading foliage detract from the beauty of the neat spreading mat-plants.

Most of these bulbous flowers (Anemones and Cyclamen are corms) are easy enough to establish beneath the low carpeting lawn plants. Bulbs—mostly Crocuses, tiny Daffodils and other miniature Narcissi—are simply put into prepared holes underneath the spreading carpets; lift up the foliage and plant the bulbs during late summer or autumn.

The leaves of Crocuses and various other early blooming bulbs grow tall and coarse and look untidy for weeks before they finally die down; so these bulbs should be grown with Thymes, for Thymes are never at their best till the summer when all the faded bulb foliage will have disappeared.

The mid-winter blooming *Crocus susianus* growing in a mass out of *Acaena microphylla* was described in chapter 2, page 39; this tiny orange flower ('Cloth of Gold Crocus') looks just as lovely too growing up through mats of the grey-green woolly Thyme mentioned above. Plant also with this lawn Thyme colonies of the earlier *Crocus imperati*, with purple fragrant flowers 3 inches tall, or the even more striking deeper purple *Var. atropurpureus*. As the foliage comes first, often early in December, it will have disappeared completely by the spring. Another beauty to grow in colonies underneath this Thyme or any flat carpeting plant is *C. sieberi*, 3 inches tall, with bright lilac flowers marked with gold.

A bulbous plant that may be grown either on its own to form a ground cover or with the creeping lawn Thymes is *Cyclamen neapolitanum*, which was described in Chapter 2. It is praised not only for its delicate rose-pink flowers but for its wonderfully attractive marbled leaves—deep green with silver streaks: leaves one would like to last permanently. Their curious beauty is enhanced by the grey-green, woolly foliage of the flowerless Thyme; furthermore the Cyclamen's flowers and leaves are tall enough to stand well above the others'. So plant beneath the white-flowered *T. drucei* 'Albus' (an inch tall and blooming in late summer), the corms of the pink Cyclamen—either the type or the rose-coloured variety *roseum* (both about 5 inches tall). You may occasionally get the pink Cyclamen mingling with the tiny white Thyme flowers; certainly you'll get the beautifully marked leaves showing up well above the flat foliage of these mat-forming plants. Underneath the crimson Thyme ('Coccineus') or the paler 'Pink Chintz' plant as many corms as you can get of the white Cyclamen *Var. album*. They are expensive but may be raised by seed (see page 59).

Heathers are usually left as plain lawn plants; for my part however I like to see a drift of white Pheasant's Eye Narcissus, *N. Poeticus* in a Heather patch—the low mat-forming varieties of *Erica carnea* are best for these tallish Narcissi. They are in full bloom by mid-April, when many of the *Carnea* deep pink Heathers are at their best.

Don't cut down the Narcissi when they have finished blooming: remove the dead flowers and let the stems and leaves die naturally. Or you may, if you wish, bend the stems and leaves down into the Heather to make them less conspicuous. Too frequent cutting back of the tops of bulbous plants ultimately weakens and ruins the bulbs.

Shrubs have been recommended for alpine lawns, but as a rule only for those that are very large. They would not only be out of place in a small lawn, but would soon cover it completely. The one mostly used is the Creeping Juniper, *Juniperus horizontalis procumbens*, which rises but 2 inches above the ground and has very attractive glaucous foliage. It may, with some care, be walked upon; but it is best not to do that when the ground beneath is hard with frost. This particular Juniper seems to do well in a variety of soils; a deeply-dug garden loam containing some sifted leafmould and a little coarse sand suits it as well as anything. The important thing is to give it plenty of room, for the branches spread out wide and root in the soil. In a cramped space this charming dwarf shrub loses much of its character.

Alpine lawns are best made in open sunny places; and, with the exception of Cyclamen which appreciate some shade, lawn plants like plenty of sun. Some however like plenty of moisture too; and the best way of providing this is to give them a place near water if you have a stream or a pond in the garden. If you haven't, it is possible to have a small artificial pool in the middle of the lawn, taking care that the surrounding ground slopes gently down to it.

It's not necessary to build a pool; glass-fibre shapes or moulds complete with ledges for moisture-loving plants, can be bought quite cheaply; and all you have to do is to dig out a hole of the requisite shape and sink the pool into it. And anyhow, if you don't like the look of the pool in your smallish alpine lawn, you can easily remove it—more quickly than you put it there.

It has been suggested that as regards providing moisture for plants growing round the edge, such a pool is practically useless, since the water cannot possibly soak through the glass-fibre and reach the roots of the plants that need it. But if the pool is surrounded by sloping ground (as I've mentioned above) moisture will naturally drain down through the soil to the plants, and furthermore during rainy spells, which occur frequently in this country, the water will rise and temporarily flood the soil and provide all the moisture necessary. The pool must of course be kept filled to the top.

The soil round natural pools and ponds and along the banks of streams is always moist and in it we can grow some very choice plants to provide drifts or mats of colour and foliage, these coming of course on the edge of the alpine lawn.

Asarum (mentioned above); the two species offered are *A. caudatum* (caudate or tail-like) and *A. europaeum*. The first, a native of California, has attractive kidney-shaped leaves, forming dense patches of green in rich moist soils; beneath the leaves come the curious flowers, three-tailed and of a brownish-red colour. The other plant, known as *Asarabacca*, is naturalized in some parts of

England; it has dark green, kidney-shaped leaves and small, nodding, purple-brown bells. Both bloom from about March to May; and both make good mat-plants for a moist shady alpine lawn.

Astilbe have feathery-looking plumes ('Goat's Beard' is the popular name) and need deep moist rich soil and some shade where possible. The two that will provide pleasant drifts of colour in the alpine lawn near water are *Astilbe simplicifolia*, a charming miniature species with white or pale pink plume flowers on stems about 6 inches tall; the leaves, deeply-divided, fern-like, are an attractive shade of green. The other is the Chinese *A. chinensis var. pumila*, with mulberry-red flowers on stems about 8 inches tall, and fern-like dark green leaves, which contrast well with the flowers. It is best in partial shade, as are all the reddish Astilbes, since the colour is toned down somewhat in subdued light. These dwarf species make charming mat plants for a moist waterside alpine lawn; the one drawback to growing them is that they are inclined to flower themselves to death. But seed is easily obtained and plenty of good healthy plants are quickly raised.

Calceolaria for the rock-garden are described in the R.H.S. Dictionary thus: 'In nature they grow for the most part in deep, cool, rather moist peaty soil, well drained, with plenty of sharp stones intermixed to ensure movement of water.' Some, like *C. polyrrhiza* (chapter 2, page 55) are well suited by the damp soil at the edge of a bog. Or the plant may be used very effectively in the alpine lawn and also in the trough or the sink garden (Chapter 6). *C. biflora* has clusters of pouched yellow flowers ¾ inch across on 4-inch stems and ovalish leaves; and *C. polyrrhiza* (page 55) is a good companion for it; both form very pleasing patches of colour in late summer. The edge of an artificial pool may not always be quite damp enough for them; but they may be grown in special soil on one of the ledges in the pool.

And these ledges are ideal for those Primulas that are found in nature actually growing in water. The best for our purpose is the little *Primula rosea* (Chapter 2, page 81) from 3 to 5 inches tall, with bright pink flowers and pale green leaves; it is very easily raised from seed; the seedlings, when big enough to handle, should be planted both *in* the pool, on the ledge or ledges, and in deep moist peaty soil round the edge. The massed pink flowers are very striking, forming a close carpet of colour in April. I've seen this Primula planted too round the edge of a shady boulder projecting well into the lawn; the plants provided a magnificent patch of deep pink in the shade; running close up to it were various kinds of carpeting Thymes.

One of the problems of making an alpine lawn is obtaining the number of plants for close planting. Close planting, as already mentioned, helps to prevent weeds from growing and seeding themselves and provides an immediate effect. Some carpeters move very slowly and take many years to cover a smallish piece of ground. Set together, say, a couple of dozen specimens of *Erica carnea* from the nurseries 6 inches apart and you have a good thick carpet of foliage and colour; the normal distance for planting these Heathers is about 12 inches apart.

In the case of Heathers, quantities of young plants are usually obtained by taking inch-long cuttings and inserting them in damp sandy peat under glass. Hundreds of young Heathers are easily raised in this way. And large numbers of plants are best obtained by cuttings. You can also raise hundreds by sowing seeds, though this is a much slower method.

With a large number of plants available—which you have raised yourself—you can afford to plant thickly. And what you don't want later on, those you have to spare after thinning out, you can give to others who are planning alpine lawns.

D.B.

Bibliography

Addisonia—New York Botanical Garden.

Alpine Garden Society—Quarterly Bulletins. London.

Bean, W. J.—*Trees and Shrubs Hardy in the British Isles.* 3 vols. New edition. London.

Botanical Magazine, The—1786 and foll.

Bowles, E. A.—*A Handbook of Crocus and Colchicum for Gardeners.* London.

Cheeseman, T. F.—*Manual of the New Zealand Flora.* Wellington, New Zealand.

Clay, S.—*The Present-day Rock Garden.* London and Edinburgh.

Corsar, K. C.—*Primulas in the Garden.* London.

Cox, E. H. M. and Stanley, Lady B.—*New Flora and Silva.* London.

Dykes, W. R.—*Genus Iris. The Handbook of Garden Irises.* London.

Engler, Dr. A. and Irmscher, Dr.—*Das Pflanzenreich.* Berlin.

Farrer, R.—*The English Rock Garden.* 2 vols. London.

Florist's Journal. 1845 and foll.

Fröderström, Dr. H.—*The Genus Sedum: A Systematic Essay.* Meddelansen frän Goteborgs Botaniska Tradgard, vols V–X, 1930–5.

Gabrielson, I. N.—*Western American Alpines.* New York.

Gray, A.—*Miniature Daffodils.* R.H.S. Daffodil Year Book, 9, 3–9, reprinted as an independent pamphlet.

Grey, C. H.—*Hardy Bulbs.* 3 vols. London.

Hall, A. D.—*The Genus Tulipa.* London.

Hornibrook, M.—*Dwarf and Slow-growing Conifers.* London.

Johnson, A. T.—*The Hardy Heaths and Some of Their Nearer Allies.* London.

Index

Index

Bellis
  perennis
    'Dresden China', 54
    'Rob Roy', 54
    rotundifolia caerulescens, 54, 137
Berberis
  Thunbergii, 152
    atropurpurea nana, 152
Betula
  nana, 152
Bolax
  glebaria, 54
Botanical Magazine, 10
Bridgeman, Charles, 10
Brown, 'Capability', 9

Calamintha
  alpina, 55, 102
  grandiflora, 55, 102
Calandrinia
  umbellata, 55, 102
    Var. '*Amaranth*', 102
Calceolaria
  biflora, 177
  polyrrhiza, 55, 56, 177
Calluna
  vulgaris, 161
    alba plena, 161
Caltha
  palustris, 24
    Var., *plena*, 24
Campanula
  alpina, 137
  arvatica, 125
cenisia, 137
  cochlearifolia, 16, 28, 155, 162,
    167
    Varieties, 163
  elatines, 137
  garganica, 102
    hirsuta var. *alba*, 156

isophylla, 137
medium, 56
persicifolia, 56
portenschlagiana, 21, 28, 102
poscharskyana, 102
pyramidalis, 56
  alba, 56
Zoysii, 57, 125, 137, 148
Campanulas for paths and steps,
  162, 163, 167
Cedrus
  libani '*Sargentii*', 152
Cerastium
  tomentosum, 32, 57
Ceratostigma
  plumbaginoides, 57, 103
Chrysanthemum
  argenteum, 57, 58
  densum, 57, 58
  amanum, 58
Cistus
  × *purpureus*, 58, 103
Clematis
  alpina, 30
Convolvulus
  cneorum, 103
  mauritanicus, 103
  tenuissimus, 104
Corydalis
  lutea, 163
Cotula
  squalida, 163, 172
Crassula
  sarcocaulis, 59
Crocus
  imperati, 18, 174
    Var. *atropurpureus*, 174
  sieberi, 18, 174
  susianus, 174
Cryptogramma
  crispa, 140

Polystichum
  setigerum var. *Plumoso-divisi-*
    lobum, 106
Pope, Alexander, 10
Potentilla
  alchemilloides, 78
  nitida, 78, 127
  verna var. *nana,* 78
Primula
  allionii, 80, 143
  auricula, 79
  boothii, 80
  denticulata, 27, 80, 159
  farinosa, 80
  forrestii, 80, 143
  gracilipes, 80
  juliae, 81
  × 'Wanda', 81
  malacoides, 143
  marginata, 112
  'Linda Pope', 112
  nutans, 80, 127
  obconica, 143
  × *pubescens,* 79, 112
  Varieties, 113
  rosea, 27, 81, 177, 178
  Var. 'Delight', 81
  rubra, 113
  sinensis, 143
  takedana, 128
  veris, 79
  Viali, 128
  vulgaris, 79, 159
  Var. *sibthorpii,* 159
Propagation, 33–6
Pulsatilla
  vernalis, 128
  vulgaris, 81

Ramonda
  myconi, 81, 113

Var., *alba,* 29
Var., *rosea,* 29
Ranunculus
  parnassifolius, 10, 129
Raoulia
  australis, 164, 173
  glabra, 156, 164, 173
  lutescens, 30, 156, 164
Repton, Humphrey, 9
Rhododendron
  camtschaticum, 82
  chryseum, 154
  ferrugineum, 9, 24
  forrestii, 23
  griersonianum, 23
  hirsutum, 9, 24
  imperator, 82
  mucronulatum, 23
  radicans, 82
  scintillans, 154
  Hybrids, 23, 82
Robinson, W., 10
Rosa
  chinensis minima, 27
  Var. 'Midget', 27, 82
  Var. 'Perla Rosa', 27

Salix
  herbacea, 154
  resticulata, 155
Santolina, 166, 167
Saponaria
  ocymoides, 13, 107, 108, 114
  Var., *alba,* 114
  Var., '*Rubra compacta*', 108
Saussurea
  stella, 144
Saxifragra
  aizoon
  Varieties, 84, 114